Lost
Leaders

Series

Volume I
Books 1, 2, and 3
Found Here

Volume II
TBD

By: Zach Graves

My Autobiographical
Whistleblower Story

Leaders Lost

The Leaders Lost logo represents the two faces of the two-faced failed leaders in this story and other leaders we might know who also failed to do the right thing shitting on those around them in the process to save their own skin. As the USNA Class of 1999 class crest states, Navigate with Honor.

The picture on the cover is of a South Korean pit viper called a Mamushi. Upon my return from investigating the MISHAP, this picture inspired my last squadron monthly safety newsletter before being fired and threatened with a psychological evaluation and FNAEB for not keeping my mouth shut by the CO and Human Factors Board. I was also told that I was emotionally unstable and unsafe/unfit to fly as an aircraft commander. Below is the excerpt from the newsletter; how true it was and still is.

Unrecognized Human Factors—Hazards that are Nowhere and Everywhere

I'm no herpetologist but being born in Arkansas and growing up in MT makes me somewhat of an authority on dangerous snakes, in my opinion. We used to have a reticulated python while I was in high school and he was mean as hell, I digress. Anyways, a parallel exists between this seemingly harmless creature and human factor hazards. This little fella, about the size of your hand spread out, is not looking for trouble. In fact he wants to have nothing to do with you, your foot or your shovel. Human factors don't go looking for us either, they are just there, like Mamushi here looking for something to eat in the drainage grate next to the road. I only spotted him once during my many walk/runs around Camp Mujok so even when you're looking they're difficult to spot. Don't let its small size be deceiving, his bite can be deadly too, they're often difficult to recognize and many times they appear invisible, only showing themselves after it's too late. An incident or MISHAP has occurred. For this reason I call them the HAZARD that is everywhere and at the same time nowhere if we're not looking for them. Since we've uncovered the danger/HAZARD, why wouldn't we be looking for them all the time now? If I didn't have an interest in snakes do you think I would've spotted Mamushi on my walk? Why would the average Sailor or Marine running around Camp Mujok think a deadly pit viper would be there next to the road? We often assume certain dangers as unlikely as they are camouflaged in the tall grass, sometimes embedded within the culture and not part of our daily ORM scan. When this happens we can be blind to our own carelessness and assumptions and not realize it, doubly concealing the hidden danger from view. "it's the way we've always done it so it must be good." Make Mamushi part of your lexicon and take Human Factor HAZARDS seriously. They *are* dangerous and *will* continue to quietly wait for us when/where we least expect them. Look twice before you step VANGUARD, read the pub or checklist twice before you do it for the first time after a long time, if you're unsure ask a question, and please apply time critical ORM in your daily activities and if you know something ain't right in how we do it, report it and get it fixed.

The goal of publishing this story and case information is to expose the truth and to finally have an open and transparent conversation about what really happened and why, and about why this information was shoved aside for so long and is only now being brought to light and adjudicated in a public forum rather than properly investigated and sufficiently acted upon during the many opportunities before when fatal catastrophe could have perhaps been stopped.

Leaders Lost is a fresh and sobering first-hand non-fiction account of one man's challenges when faced with reprisal being forced upon him by his aviation squadron CO and further exacerbated by a negligent Navy, government IG, congressional office, and several other Shipmates who stood by while it happened. The scene of the story takes place over the course of about eight years and documents his journey through the trials and tribulations of backstabbing, bureaucratic nonsense, and the twilight zone of reasonably good people insisting upon knowing what the right thing is to do and then doing the exact opposite. Leaders Lost represents a play on words where the Leaders that became Lost for political reasons and not having a spine directly contributed to the decisions and conditions set into motion which led to some incredible Leaders actually being Lost in unnecessary and preventable aircraft MISHAPS. His vitriol towards detrimental status quo and those that support it refreshes the instincts to once again question authority especially when it's tough. At its heart however the story shows the importance of believing in yourself, not giving up, and trusting in those that help and support you to get you through the hard times.

Clarence Zachary Graves retired on 1June2019 after serving 20 years on active duty in the United States Navy. He still works for the government as an analyst, planner, and executive team builder.

Leaders Lost

A Lesson in
Good Leadership
vs
Bad Leadership

And
Understanding How to
Prevent
The Unfortunate
From Happening to You

And
Being Able to
Recognize
When You Are Dealing with A__-Holes
&
What to Do

And
The Struggle for Truth, or at Least the Most Correct Version of It

By: Clarence Zachary Graves, LCDR USN (ret)

In the Spirit of

Tecumseh,

Samuel Saunders and his wife Pashika,

Adam Brown Sr. and his wife, Adam Brown Jr. and Theressa Brown,

Quindaro Nancy Brown and Abelard Guthrie,

Abalura Guthrie and Clarence Graves,

And the other Shawnee, Wyandotte, and Cherokee,

Also The Hart's, The Brandenburg's, The Hollis', The Springer's, The

O'Connor's, The Griffith's, The Swope's, The Worfel's, The Clark's,

The Sourbeer's, and the Webb's

Special mention to

My family and friends

Who keep me going every day

In memory of

Montana

Where my heart is

For

My Dad

Supporting Reference [1]: Organized by Chronology, Complaint Submission, and Appendix by Book Volume

"Leaders Lost" - <u>Leaders Lost Series, Book 3</u>

2020
Manuscript and publishing proposal   p. 10-105, 107
FOIA correspondence and USNI correspondence   p. 108-113
Final BCNR response letter   p. 114 [2017 first BCNR response letter p. 547]

2019
BCNR correspondence p. 118
Copyright Office correspondence p. 123
[Retirement 31May2019] and Misc Congressional correspondence Tester, Daines p. 125

Appendix B— - <u>Leaders Lost Series, Book 2</u>
Government record of reviewed files

FOIA public record (recv'd Apr2020)
        File 1   p. 129
        File 2   p. 157
        File 3   p. 160
        File 4   p. 171

Books 1 & 2 are free to the public to read at
www.goodleaderslost.com

Appendix A— - <u>Leaders Lost Series, Book 1</u>
Submitted Case Material to IG and BCNR

2018
3. Third Congressional Inquiry request letter dtd 8May2018   p. 543
        BCNR request DD Form 149 dtd 8May2018
        BCNR reconsideration letter dtd 5Apr2018
        Senator Daines response letter dtd 10Apr2018
        [2017] BCNR panel disposition letter dtd 5Sep2017

2017
2. Second Congressional Inquiry request letter dtd 6Dec2017   p. 549
        My continued testimony and history of my case
        [2016] First Congressional Inquiry response correspondence dtd 26May2016-5Sep2017
        Pictures of me and my family

2016
1. First Congressional Inquiry dtd 26May2016 and sixteen enclosures including initial complaint
p. 554 (Tester), 562 (Daines), 570 (Zinke), 578 (McCain), 586 (Reed), 594 (ASD OLA)

2012
0. Initial Reprisal Complaint dtd 2Dec2012 and twenty three enclosures   p. 609

2011
Supporting Reference [2]: VulcanEx 12-1 After Action Report

<u>Leaders Lost Manuscript Table of contents</u> - <u>Leaders Lost Series, Book 3</u>

Books 1 & 2 are free to the public to read at
www.goodleaderslost.com

Leaders Lost Series, Book 1

Monthly Safety Reports Contents and Enclosures (included)

Leaders Lost Series, Book 3

Forward

Let me be clear this manuscript, not the reports, is not a professional work the way it is written. It is fraught with emotion and frustration and sharing of my experience internally and externally of the situation over roughly eight years of dealing with the fallout of a safety and professional situation at the squadron and complaint I submitted in response. While everything here is still non-fiction and based on fact as I reported and recollect, the reason I wrote this style of manuscript was simply because the copyright office would not honor my complaint materials as an original work so I had no choice but to re-capture my experience in clearly a less formal manner. I did try and organize the material the best I could so the reader and researcher or student could digest the volume of information more easily. After beginning to write it all down again and organize the information in this manner I found the process and experience to be very therapeutic in letting go to a certain extent. I think the expletives helped too.

It's a funny thing looking back. I just finished writing the major portions of the story. I wonder if I got it right, captured everything correctly, told the story in a useful and accurate manner? It all started out as a choice while safety officer at the squadron. What was I going to do with the story and information that was unfolding before me? Should I keep my mouth shut which so many others had done in safety before me? Maybe they spoke out to some extent but quickly withdrew for one reason or another. I chose not to withdraw but continue doing my job and then had to decide when doing my job got more difficult whether I would speak out to make my points known. When speaking out became more difficult I had to decide whether to withdraw or fight. What was the right thing and should I have done things differently? Did I have a choice whether to speak out or not, and if my only choice was to speak out was there any other more constructive way to do it differently that may have avoided the situation I claim to have taken place? What is my culpability in all this? I think we all have choices to make and the others that I describe who were involved simply made theirs, and I made mine, and here we are. I'm still curious to know the full truth behind some of their decisions and to what extent the higher chain of command was involved. I refuse to accept in this case that it's just the way things are and you're

screwed if you do and you're screwed if you don't. Ironically, as events unfold across the government

and in the military dealing with COVID-19 I again see a lot of parallels and similarities with people trying

to speak up and do the right thing in government only to get shot in the back of the head ie.**CVN CO**.

These issues are appearing in and being questioned and discussed at the latest press conference I saw

***ex pres** give on 6 April and so glaringly evident in the behavior of the acting SECNAV. I so want

to believe that everything we learned about good leadership and doing the right thing wasn't just lip

service at the Academy and during my time in the Navy. I like to believe that this story is an extension of

that best practice of doing the hard thing in the service to your country despite all your instincts and

people around you telling you "No." I like to believe that my friends and family will view me and my

character in a way that is true and representative of reality, in a manner that gives them comfort and pride

in knowing somebody they know is out there fighting the good fight and stands for that which is good,

and that will not be swayed by the temptation of power and control, to do the right thing and stay in the

batter's box and keep on trying to the very end no matter how sick and tough the pitches are—I refuse to

accept defeat, I refuse to strike out, I will keep on trying until I get a hit and my voice is finally heard and

the problems properly addressed and rectified. I'm lucky that I always had great coaches standing by me

in the dugout to lend a hand when you find yourself in that funk and you can't find your way out. May

not be pretty what they tell you but at least you know you're getting the honest truth and genuine desire

they want to see you hit a home run some day and win the game.

    I wrote this before sharing with the others who I would've liked to also share their thoughts and

perspective on the story and maybe even share their own story as well. I hope they still do. If they

choose not to then I hope I'm able to move forward just as well and I hope I represent them in an accurate

and respectful manner.

    My initial reporting was meant to be very objective and analytical as much absent from

emotional decision making as possible and little to no subjective conclusions. I wanted to present as

much fact as possible as the foundation of whatever story that I was going to unravel. I tried to continue

this method

into the complaint process as much as possible and I think I did initially. My later complaints began to

show more emotion while trying to connect the dots of the case in a precise manner back to the facts as

much as possible in an organized manner. Once it became clear that it didn't matter how the facts were

presented and that the judgement wasn't going to change no matter the correct circumstance or how well I

made the case, then I got much more abrupt and disrespectful at times to properly express the true nature

of how I was feeling and how the situation was affecting me but also to lend a more open and expressive

tone to the story. For some reason, people don't like facts as much as they like drama, controversy, and a

good old cockfight—"are you not entertained?" as Maximus in The Gladiator said it. He died in the end

so maybe not the best example. Nonetheless, I recognize my final presentation of this story, even though

I feel like I've told it over and over again several times in multiple submissions, is very emotional,

personally revealing, and maybe even seem to be exaggerated at certain points since I wrote it from pure

memory for events and feelings that occurred many years ago. I want to share the burden of all this with

you now, and I hope it will better prepare you and maybe offer some perspective for the many burdens

you too will face in your life.

Am I broken or damaged from all this? Yes a little. Do I regret any of it, No. Do I think writing

this will solve anything, No. Do I think writing this was necessary? Yes. Do I think this message will

help people now and in the future cope with similar situations they may be dealing with? Yes. Would I

recommend others in similar situations to speak out in the same manner as I did and go to such lengths as

to write this story? Yes. If you feel your story is strongly substantiated, has merit, and has factual

evidence to support your claim, absolutely I think you should report it and fight for your story to be told.

In the absence of concrete evidence, he said she said, I still think the story is worth reporting but I've no

confidence any authority will bother looking into it. I felt like I had a strong case and I got shot down at

every level to be heard and break through. Nobody is going to fight harder for your story to be told than

you, unfortunately. The laws and regulations are supposed to be in place so that your voice and you are

protected but reality shows us that this isn't always the case so if you do plan to speak out then you'd

better get ready for a fight. Very seldom you will have a coalition behind you saying, "Hey that's great, of course we were breaking the law and going against written policy and standards and this person should get a medal for telling on us, congratulations!" Even though it's actually everybody's job to look out for this and prevent this especially under the special circumstances prescribed in the law, do not expect a warm reception when you blow the whistle on your organization, your boss, or other employees. You are an outcast now, you'll need to own it.

Many people I went to Boat School with were perpetrators and chose to stand idly by, so why? Did they justify their actions and decisions as supporting the greater good and therefore the ends justified the means? I did not think them to be "bad" people. I said before that I always tried to understand how seemingly good intelligent people could be responsible for and make decisions which perpetrate such bad and clearly preventable outcomes? Everybody has reasons for doing the things they do. I have my reasons for doing this which I think I make pretty clear at many different points. I wish I could understand the reasons why these individuals chose to perpetuate going against established policy and in the face of knowingly doing wrong still chose to perpetuate acts and culture of malfeasance, hostility, dysfunction, and fear within the squadron. Maybe they were scared too and just couldn't be big enough to stand up against it. Maybe from their vantage point everything was great so why rock the boat. I'm still fascinated by the simple conclusion that regardless of everybody's reasons for doing or not doing certain things in this situation, the right thing to do was to speak out and expose the wrong doing. I'm equally fascinated by the resistance in the system of people and process that protected the opposite.

I waited until I retired to begin trying to organize my materials into a book. The Navy waited until after I retired to complete the final adjudication of my BCNR request, the final notch in the coffin I figured where I could no longer pursue any fight through the government or regulatory process. I felt like I had taken that effort as far as I could. I did receive my last notification of the results though which indicated that my case would now fall under FOIA so maybe I had achieved a little of something making it subject to public record for review. For good measure I submit my story along with the FOIA materials I received for final comparison. Copyright shot me down on my original submission of my report organized into a book. I had to re-write my submission into more of an original work and not a collection of papers as they put it even though I felt like it was already an original work compiled over many years. So I started writing this manuscript to further get the materials and thoughts off my chest. This process overall has made me feel very relieved with some sense of closure. Not ironically I still feel like I have to watch my back as I continue trying to speak out about these things and what happened to me, what I experienced, how it affected me, and what I've observed through this process. It took me a long time but I finally reached out to Nicole for her feelings on the matter and was pleasantly surprised of her enthusiasm towards the idea of this. After watching Tiger King during my quarantine I was reminded I might still have to watch my step though because who might be waiting patiently for me to misstep and take that wrong step in how I approach this issue of speaking out in the manner of a book. How do I publish? I thought USNI was the best option for several reasons. CYA for legal purposes to start but also I felt would lend a genuine sense of validity to the story, this is a Navy story for others to learn from. I feel sad that this process is the last resort and only way the Navy is able to learn from its mistakes, but I suppose at least it finally worked and they heard what I've been saying for many years. Still not confident the Navy, DoD, or government will actually listen, understand, and be part of the change process and solutions. Maybe our future leaders and you will listen too. Will this be taught and the structure of the story converted into a leadership and safety curriculum? It's almost one year after I retired and I'm finally ready to stop telling this story and let the words of these pages take it over for me.

Leaders Lost 31Jan2020

Preface

I have something to say on the subject. Some will flow while some may sound whiny. Some of the way it's written may not perfectly line up with the supporting reference and parts and pieces may bounce around a bit as I went from memory as best I could from my recollection of events and detail. If you prefer to use FOIA, request BCNR Docket #s 4304-18 and 8863-16 and IG case #'s 201602083 and 201300109. I wanted this to be more feeling and substantive and less factually based in formality the way it's written and organized. I mean to be scornful and sound scornful because I think that element of my experience is most important now to come through in the story and the writing. I want the reader to know how this has impacted me personally then and over the years and what I really think about the situation and the people involved. To be in this situation and to heal and move on requires us to be angry about what transpired and at times, frequently, be pissed off. Many times you have no choice but to bury it and focus on what you have to do to get through right then in the moment, and many times that's what people are left with. Going crazy will not erase your pain nor anger so I chose to write it down. I want to continue speaking out about the story, and my scorn, to let people know that this is not O.K., what they (my CO and others) did and how the government supported it is not O.K., the people involved that chose to remain silent is not O.K., but that you are O.K. even if you don't feel so, and that understanding that honest mistakes by people are O.K. but intentional mistakes of malfeasance and abuse of power is NOT— and is illegal and needs to be prosecuted especially if supported at the highest levels. The supporting reference [1] focuses on the details and facts, so you should cross reference what you want and tell me where I'm wrong or inconsistent. I'm confident though that the facts and my record speak for themselves so enjoy my story as a very quick snapshot of time and space (roughly 8 yrs), I have to move on as best I can and let my story here take over and carry the lessons and my pain into the wind. If you're a critic I'll meet you on the wrestling mat any time. I'm not a novelist so bear with me. I gave the Navy ample opportunity to properly adjudicate my claims. I've given the government now ample opportunity as a whole to properly investigate and adjudicate my claims. I don't fuck around. Unless I'm naked in bed with my wife I don't like to fuck around. I'll play politics all day long but as soon as the claim on my

bosses end arose that I was crazy (emotionally unstable, threatening me with FNAEB and psychological

evaluation if I do not comply) and that was somehow the reason for how I was behaving, or not behaving,

and that somehow could be used to discredit me and my reporting, that's when I knew I had to fight the

fuck back. The normal processes of a department head or anybody really in an aviation squadron (any

government body) should not have to go to those lengths or endure this type of ridicule to correct

grievances and take action on clear acts of misconduct by unit leadership and personnel. If I did and was

doing the right thing then fucking come out and say it and get behind me!

In 2012 I officially became a government whistleblower for safety related protected

communications I'd been making during my time as a department head at HM-14. Although the

government determined my complaint was invalid, I can say with specificity that my safety reporting was

100% accurate and that as a result I faced retaliation for the information I'd been aggressively trying to

communicate, investigate, and bring to light. My goal in doing this has always been to fix the problems

and underlying causes in leadership, culture, and loss of ethical fortitude by many within the government

particularly the CO, XO, department heads, and many other community leaders. As a direct result of their

individual and collective failures we lost people and equipment to preventable MISHAPS. My critics will

be quick to point out that I didn't really blow the whistle on anything because they already knew

everything that was going on and that my reporting was simply an extension of course corrections they'd

already started to implement. I simply failed at playing the game everybody else was playing they might

say. They might say that the reason I chose such an abrupt and loud approach to speaking out and

rocking the boat is because I was just making waves to improve my beleaguered position as a struggling

department head. Once this is published as my final report on the matter they might finish with this as

being simply a continuation of that struggling effort to get noticed and recognized for something I've no

business taking credit for or speaking about because I'm a nobody and don't have any clue the big picture

of what I'm talking about.

Please don't give me credit for anything. In my position as Safety Officer and even today I continue to believe that if only people had somebody to take the first step in speaking out then they'd rally and get behind them regardless of how hard or scary the results might be. I was wrong about that though at least as far as I can tell. There was no rally. This has been hard to endure emotionally and certainly scary at certain points taking on the establishment and putting yourself and family at some unknown risk. That is a good question though, why can't I just let this go and why do I continue to feel compelled to keep this going towards some kind of closure? The truth is that I don't really know why I keep pushing this and insist on blowing the whistle on something that is already well known. What I continue to feel strongly about that in my opinion has not been properly and adequately adjudicated is the issue surrounding my case involving reprisal. I guess I am just self-serving like everybody else. Nobody appears to dispute the safety reporting regardless of who when and how it came to light, but I don't believe the government in this case has taken proper responsibility in the clear and convincing reprisal against me as a result of that situation nor has the government allowed the investigative process to hold leadership accountable. Once again, I've not been found at fault for any of my reporting or for continuing to be outspoken—In fact my efforts have been validated through several independent reports. What hasn't been litigated are the actions which I experienced against me designed and with intent to stifle my reporting, discredit me and my reporting, intimidate and threaten and bully me in the workplace, and specifically intent on damaging my career. Although focusing on the FITREP took up a lot of bandwidth in the process as a key consideration of reprisal, it actually only involved a small piece of the story albeit an important one with respect to timing of the complaint process. In other circumstances I'd say that to be in any aviation squadron you have to have pretty thick skin and being in the military you have to simply accept that you get your ticket punched and move up when your told to do so regardless of your personal thoughts on the matter however, I felt that these fuckers knew exactly what they were trying to do (for which they've succeeded up to this point) and why—maintain a hostile work environment and perpetuate a culture of fear and intimidation, direct improper and illegal maintenance scheduling and actions, turn a blind eye to the results, cover their ass and make sure to inflict improper disproportionate unfair illegal professional pain on me and my family in the process, or anyone else for that matter who might speak out against them. Well done assholes! Therefore, I will not let this go and will continue to speak out now more publicly to further expose that leadership was clearly aware of the safety and cultural dysfunction which led to loss of aircraft, equipment, and the unnecessary deaths of several people, and I will continue to speak out to correct these errors. I also intend to further shed light on the unfair personnel actions that were taken against me as a result which have since then significantly impacted me personally and professionally. Lastly, I'd like to continue to put a spotlight on the actions and decisions surrounding my case by the Navy and DoD IG and BCNR with regard to the mishandling of my case, thwarting its investigation, and covering up material evidence and witnesses.

Specifically:

-Having me sign an invalid non-disclosure agreement which the Navy JAG office determined they'd never seen anything like it before; it didn't even provide a date of termination

-Never giving me an opportunity to make an appearance

-Not providing a waiver for the 60 day reporting requirement

-Not considering all the unfair personnel actions in the preliminary inquiry

-Not investigating the case or reopening the case when new evidence was provided against the reasons for not doing a full investigation in the first place

-Having witnesses not communicate with me or provide evidence

-Navy IG directing me to wait to submit my initial complaint for evidentiary reasons and then have those reasons for waiting become the primary reason for not investigating the case for not meeting the 60 day reporting requirement

-Doing whatever they could to exploit loopholes or loose interpretations to avoid having to investigate and reopen the case

-Not fully considering all the evidence by the BCNR in the context of the case and its impacts on my career through my FITREPS and overall loss of professional opportunities as a result

-Not providing me with some level of return to wholeness as a result of the governments mistreatment of me through the circumstances from the squadron, the initial complaint, and follow-on complaint

I'll also point out that the congressional inquiry turned out to be a complete waste of time and that "inquiry" simply meant in this case a question between staffers about what was going on, not any sort of directing or leading an investigation about what was going on or transpiring with respect to the full context of the case that I'd provided several offices. I don't think the policies or whistleblower programs are at fault, I think the people in charge of them collectively failed from the bottom all the way to the top, hence I find myself here sharing this with you.

Introduction

My name is Clarence Zachary Graves. I'm 43 years old. I've been married about 18 years. My wife and I have three kids.

I was born in Springdale, AR and raised in Billings, MT. I can no longer say whether my upbringing was normal—normal to what? I enjoyed my childhood. I left for college at the Naval Academy when I was 18 thinking I knew much more about the world than I actually did but was determined to face whatever life had in store head-on. I spent four years there toiling about my studies and doing my best at pole-vault. I met my wife during my second year and she straightened me out, somewhat. I was able to graduate after finishing first semester with a 0.8 and reported to flight school in the winter.

I'm leaving out quite a bit from my formative years but fast forward to 2010 I found out I'd been selected to return to flying as an Operational Department Head while I was finishing my tour in Germany. I was pretty excited and surprised too because I'd already been passed over once and seldom did anybody make it on the second look. I was considered in community circles as off-track meaning the path for professional development I pursued was not the traditional pedigree boards looked at for being career enhancing as an aviator. This didn't bother me about the system, that's just the way it was; there is always a penalty for doing what you want to do and trying to put your family first; can't waste time being a hater of a system you volunteered for. I'd done well everywhere I went but I was not the best. I also did not try and overtly kiss ass and back-stab to get ahead which you need to master to some extent. I wanted my best to be enough and didn't want to get ahead through sleight of hand or other illusion of character; if I failed that was O.K. too as long as I understood the decision I was making and was being honest with myself and those around me. The military among other teams is built on trust and if I couldn't accept what I had to do then I'd walk away. This case was different, this wasn't typical business, and the reprisal was very personal in nature, targeted, calculated, manipulative, and intentional. I think you'll find that I was just doing a good job, leadership started not to like it, and these efforts were an attempt to shut me down. I remember right before he fired me as Safety Officer at the end of the formal counseling session he said to me that if I wanted to pursue an IG inspection then I should "go ahead" but that I wouldn't be doing it as Safety Officer. Among everything else this told me that he knew exactly what he was doing and why he was doing it. What did he tell investigators or what did I leave out that somehow outweighed everything I'd presented? I guess we'll never know, but at least I can say after all this that my integrity is still intact. That detail was very important to me.

I'm starting to ramble, what does this have to do with anything? Well I've had many tests in my life but the story I'm telling you here describes one of my toughest. To a large extent personally I'm still being graded and probably always will be; did I do the right thing—am I still doing the right thing? I think I did, but after all this time and having to think about it so much internally sometimes you wonder otherwise. Sometimes anger is all you can think about, sometimes you're depressed, sometimes you don't know how you feel, sometimes you felt so isolated and alone you can't figure out why doing the right thing should be so hard—why is nobody else helping and how the fuck do the people in charge get away with this shit?

Here's the best recollection of empirical facts I can give you from my experience and the data I collected from several independent sources and methods. The results I believe show that enlisted and officer leadership knew and understood the gravity of the situation and what was going on and that, while I may not go as far to say that any of them intended for bad things to happen, their direct behavior decisions and attitudes in support of individual and collective cultural mores did directly result in MISHAPs of equipment and most regrettably unnecessary deaths of friends and shipmates. I cannot explain these results except to say that what transpired is basic human behavior—self-preservation, but what I'm confident about the results in is that they show Leaders became Lost somehow along the way and hence some of our best Leaders were Lost to unnecessary and preventable tragedy as a result.

That charge only covers the safety related information. What I also charge and feel very strongly about whether right or wrong is that leadership also knew and understood what I was trying to do and why in my safety reporting, they tried to manipulate information and change the narrative to make suggestions about me and my performance that weren't accurate, they slandered my character and made false accusations about my fitness for duty on the ground and in the air, and they intentionally ranked me and evaluated my performance in a less than optimal way to hurt me professionally as a direct result of my reporting and speaking up, not directly related to an observed or properly measured poor performance or proper comparison with my peers. This is where I differ from what I said above about accepting a process that I volunteered to support in that I think the record supports with enough evidence that their collective actions towards me were well outside the acceptable and allowable standards (regardless of how could be strictly interpreted to stay within regulatory standards) and that these actions were instead clearly punishments and attempts to gag my reporting as a whistleblower to conceal their own failures, crimes, and the true nature of the toxic leadership, safety, and maintenance culture that existed. What transpired was bad for everybody—and deadly. I tried to begin identifying and reporting errors and connecting the dots of what was going on and understanding "why" as early on as possible; I developed a communication strategy to effectively report up the chain and around the squadron giving them all the benefit of the doubt that maybe somehow they didn't already know. Lastly, I attempted to singularly (since I found nobody else would speak up) hold them to account when the worst (but foreseen and predictable) began to occur by not allowing them all to hand-waive or minimalize the true nature of what was going on within the collective heart of the squadron (later to be discovered within the collective heart of the community) as not directly tied to the MISHAPS that were occurring. I thought to myself when resistance occurred to putting obvious causal facts into the safety investigation—I would think to myself, "Am I the crazy one here, why is this so tough when clearly we as a squadron and safety team have been (in my mind) been so aggressively accounting for and reporting these types of errors in safety and maintenance behaviors and leadership decision-making since I started the job?" Unfortunately my commanding officers and other department heads all disagreed with me, the Navy IG and DoD IG disagreed with me, and the Bureau of Corrections to Naval Records (BCNR) disagreed with me (twice), so my track record apparently in being able to successfully report this information and my alleged charges has not been too good. My Congressional representatives and others on the Defense committees helped very little to look into anything let alone push for investigating the case. So that's why I'm writing this— here you go—so you can make your own decisions, understand and take a look at what was really going on behind the scenes, and if nothing else learn something from the information I provide and the story behind it. It still frustrates me though that when behind closed doors or off the record, everybody who chose to remain silent seemed to agree with me and come clean.

So that was basically how I'd describe my time at the squadron, not a typical or desirable Department Head tour for me professionally, personally, or for my family although I did leave feeling partially satisfied that I did my best and I was doing the right thing by filing the complaint. Was it necessary to file the complaint as reprisal? Would I have also filed a whistleblower complaint just for the safety information by itself if they'd left me and my career development alone? Well I don't know really but I think I reached a point in the process of reporting where you couldn't separate the two—what I was reporting and how I found myself being forced to aggressively report it and account others for the information was quickly followed by the more aggressive negative response I received as a result. I suppose if they had just said, "Hey you're doing a great job, just keep doing what you're doing and we'll support every effort you make to run this up the flagpole because this is that important and we see now and understand why it's so important because of the connections you've/we've identified between our collective behaviors, attitudes, and decisions and the recent MISHAPS in the squadron and greater so within the community—it makes sense now." Earlier-on I think for the most part I was prepared to just part ways and cry "uncle" but after the MISHAPS started happening things started to get ugly and it became apparent that the toxicity of the culture in all respects was so hardened within the arteries of the squadron and the community that there was no going back if my intention was to see this through and make the necessary changes stick. While much has been done I still think there is a lot of plasticity left within those veins despite these efforts and others to root out the bad actors and replace bad practices with good within the cultural norms. I'm pretty confident there are many out there, former colleagues included, who read this and say, "He's full of shit and I can't believe he had the balls to report let alone publish this shit." My simple response is that "you all" (whoever that is—you know who you are) are the ones who put me in the position but to have no choice but to report this shit—so fuck you assholes! My continued efforts to speak out in this manner now is an extension of that and recognition that a bad system of human behavior will always return if continued efforts aren't made to resist and prevent it. What is my interest now, being that there is always an ulterior motive presented by the other side if you don't first—I want to make something right out of something that I observed, witnessed, and experienced to be terribly wrong, and I want this message and story to help educate others in the process to prevent it from happening in the future through training and awareness of the signs. I'd also prefer others won't have to go through what I have in this endeavor but unfortunately human nature again will always require individual efforts to help speak out against it and correct the wrongs. Mostly I hope that our friends and family don't lose their lives unnecessarily due to highly preventable circumstances that we as people and personalities created, instead of a bonafide conflict against a dangerous adversary. We should aim not be our own most dangerous adversary.

A counter-narrative I constantly would hear from people, and suspect still exists, related to how we accept risk in training is that the mission was *operational necessity* and had to happen. If you look-up and understand the definition you'd see it doesn't have any part in a training environment at all and in an operational context is only used in the most extreme circumstances to convey the importance of the mission so at our squadron not forward deployed, trying to convince me something is operational necessity doesn't really hold water—particularly in reference to flying aircraft out of the area for a hurricane or HURREX as we call it or the usual training missions or maintenance flight. I was told I'm risk averse for seeing things this way.

Another false narrative in my humble opinion (since that is all this is really, right?) is that even though things weren't the way they were supposed to be in terms of programmatics, policy, and standard operating procedures, and specific commander's guidance even orders (meaning normalization of non-standard unapproved practices) so in essence the *wrong way* in all respects becomes the *right way*, some people at the squadron believed that since we all knew about it and since we were all accepting the same risk in how we were doing business (the wrong way) that therefore it was O.K., and now it had official approval or simply now became an approved process. I had an individual at the squadron after I left and after my friend Wes died say to me that, while unfortunate, Wes was one of the high flight time pilots so he knew and understood the risk the same as everybody else—basically saying that "shit" happens and if Wes was really concerned about what was going on he shouldn't have been flying around so much like he didn't give a shit or that everything was O.K. His comment also indicated to me that at least from his perspective understanding the risk meant that the substance behind it was well known by everybody about the state of things, how things were being done operationally in gross error, and the decisions behind the scenes that went along with it to conceal the truth; I didn't see this risk being reported up the chain as a clear matter of understanding and reflection of what that truly meant. This was difficult to listen to after the fact but I think it conveys a prevailing sentiment about how people approached attitudes in the squadron; you were either with the status quo of doing business or you weren't. There wasn't any middle ground and the standard was that set by the status quo instead of by what was right or by approved standardized and official published policy.

Unfortunately the journey wasn't over and what began to unravel after my time at the squadron was just the beginning. The journey I'm about to take you on now in my writing is not very sexy and may seem very boring at times, maybe even sound like I'm complaining as a distraught victim. Well you're right, the story does sound like that at times and unfortunately that is the life of a whistleblower trying to do the right thing because you wouldn't be a whistleblower and telling the story in this fashion if the principle governing body wasn't against you in the narrative. I believe though that you will find and maybe even agree with me that the facts line up; I've yet been privy to the counter-argument from the government because no investigation was conducted and the individuals in question at all levels have never had to answer for anything. For me however, I feel like I've been under constant investigation for the entire time since I spoke out and will continue to be through the publishing of this manuscript and supporting report and evidence.

Before I get into the detailed analysis of my…. analysis, I want to clarify a few points. First, the IG preliminary inquiry that I was led to believe was supposed to be a full investigation took about three years to complete which I thought odd that it took them that long to arrive at the simple conclusion which was that they would not pursue a full investigation. Also odd, I thought, was the reason they didn't pursue a full investigation was because of a 60 day statutory reporting requirement (which I'll address later) and not because of not finding sufficient evidence, validation, and merit to the case. At the end of the day, all my arguments were unsuccessful at changing the decision to not investigate my case and therefore I had to decide to walk away, present new evidence, or pursue a congressional inquiry and a BCNR. I was told that if I wanted the IG to consider re-opening my case I would need to submit new evidence that supported my complaint. This seemed problematic since I thought I'd submitted the most compelling case I could and what else could there possibly be that I left out that could be more convincing? Was I not saying the magic word or saying things in just the right way to trigger the necessary response. It seemed like the whole time they were just paying lip service and going through the motions but there was never any real intent to investigate or see through the details and full scrutiny that my complaint and associated reporting had to offer. In addition, I was trying to validate my own argument for a case that the IG didn't invalidate, just that the case didn't move forward because of the time constraint in which the complaint was submitted.

So second, after being notified my case would not be investigated due to the 60 day requirement not being met (three years after the fact) I attempted to argue unsuccessfully the following additional details which they still refused to accept as valid for reopening the case. I argued that my FITREP and how it was characterized against me in the full context of the situation *did* qualify in regards to an unfair personal action of reprisal (fancy lingo for reprisal cases) so the 60 day requirement *was* met. I also argued that they the IG (without explanation) omitted the consideration of my flight time waiver letter as a targeted and Unfair Personnel Action (UPA) taken against me which my initial complaint included and that which would also have allowed the 60 day requirement to be met. I also argued that even if the 60 day requirement wasn't met (missed by only a few days of the last identified UPA in the preliminary inquiry) that there was sufficient evidence, validation, and merit to the case as shown through the complaint and the preliminary inquiry to waive the 60 day requirement, which the IG rejected multiple times. I also argued that I had begun communicating the merits of my complaint and my case in terms of protected communications to official reporting representatives by consulting AIRLANT IG **Mr. 5** and NCIS **Special Agent 6** well before I submitted the official complaint. I also argued that I submitted the complaint to **Mr. 5*** under his direction to wait until after I received the FITREP, which didn't happen until several weeks later… I'm repeating what I said in my earlier reporting, at the end of the day, all my arguments were unsuccessful at changing the decision to not re-open and investigate my case and therefore I had to decide to walk away, present new evidence, or pursue a congressional inquiry and a BCNR. I began to see that there was clear intent and efforts being taken to not re-open nor investigate the case I'd brought forward. I wanted to know why and furthermore still wanted my case to be fully investigated and wholeness of the situation restored or remedied in some way.

I promise to eventually apply more structure to the story, but just real quick—there's lots of tangents to take away from the focus but sometimes I think they add to the context. I'm not perfect, as a person, officer, nor pilot—I've got more skeletons than a cemetery. I don't think I'm trying to be holier than thou. My true friends know deep down I'm pretty shy and don't like being flashy, bragging, or out in the spotlight. I guess what I'm trying to say is that I'd rather not be doing this unless I felt compelled that I absolutely had to. I don't think anybody wants to be in this position. Contrary to one of the prevailing opposition narratives that this individual is just a disgruntled employee looking for attention, a trouble maker. I find that as a whistleblower I am constantly defending myself and more importantly the burden falls on me to convince the IG and everybody else that there is a case, with sufficient cause and evidence, to investigate the situation and the people involved. I always thought the purpose of the investigation would be to gather all the relevant evidence to fully understand the situation and then determine if there is a valid case or not. Well, no investigation was ever done so this again, is what I'm left with.

I probably don't need to but I will anyway draw a connection to LT Wes Vandorn's efforts to report these issues prior to the MISHAP that took his life and several of his crew with him. His wife and family continue to this day to celebrate his life. His family's efforts particularly Nicole continue to shed light on the work and problems he was attempting silently to reveal and correct. I considered Wes a good friend, somebody with solid character who I could count on at the squadron. We had in common during this time while I was the Safety Officer observing and reporting everything from the outside of the programs, Wes was very actively involved inside the maintenance programs and within the upcoming leadership circles of the squadron. Everybody liked him and respected him as an Officer, pilot and friend. He and several of his crew died in a crash roughly one year after I left in 2013. I did not realize the extent of what he was gathering and silently reporting until after his death. The details of which are all well documented in the movie and other reports that his wife helped produce. A few things stand out here. First, Wes was not afraid of a challenge and definitely not afraid to speak his mind and speak out. He was intelligent and well organized. When he set his sights and mind to something he did it and followed through. So I was very surprised and not surprised to find out the extent of what he was doing behind the scenes. I was surprised because that approach did not seem to be in his nature to not be more outspoken. Early on when I was conducting my own investigations he actually seemed pretty outspoken and vocal about what was going on and how he was trying to correct deficiencies in leadership and programmatics. He was the most outspoken and detailed during the safety investigation interview he gave in Korea. All his information gathered and analysis was apparently incredibly detailed and thorough just done so without apparently anybody knowing about it except in the personal context with his wife and family and some others that he trusted. Something seemed to change after I left; I don't recall having any communication with Wes directly prior to his death but I know he was aware of my situation and my complaint after I left. One of my biggest fears I put in my complaint before leaving the squadron was the culture of fear that existed around speaking out about the status quo around the squadron. It was a career killer (no pun intended) to go against the grain or be cast as an outsider. I told the command and the IG that I thought these conditions existed and that this toxic atmosphere would prevent others from speaking out simply by viewing or hearing about what people were observing happening to me as a department head not to mention the Safety Officer. I cannot say for certain this had anything to do with Wes keeping things behind the scenes but either he made that decision because he observed what would happen to him if he didn't or he was working behind the scenes with many others in the squadron in a silent nature who never came forward or came out in support of my case. Of course I'll never know whether they just stayed silent or whether they were never asked any questions by the IG. Either way, the apparent lack of transparency and openness by (Wes) the most fervent and aggressive leadership, safety, and compliance champions I knew as a colleague and friend felt compelled to approach his reporting in silence.

The second connection has to do with the causal factors of his crash. The safety report is out there I believe in the public and since I wasn't there I cannot say any of my hypothesis are for certain. I believe though that the information Wes and I were making separate but seemingly parallel attempts to highlight and expose directly contributed to the MISHAP that took his life. I believe the community leadership failures and attitudes surrounding this time period were negligent in taking seriously what was being reported from my complaint (assuming people were aware) and other independent internal command investigations going on. I think that some would present the counter-argument that the community just didn't connect the dots in time to break-up the Swiss cheese from aligning but I contend that the community and other leadership involved were directly stifling our efforts to prevent the catastrophe by raising awareness of the situation and shedding light on the right path.

I told leadership what was going on, I believe Wes was also telling leadership, leadership knew and chose not to do anything about it so please stop trying to sell to everyone that these MISHAPS are just flukes, random occurrences and not connected in any way. If leadership didn't know, then these individuals are just as negligent because the information was there and they chose to ignore it or look the other way. They are all connected by systemic leadership failures supporting a culture of non-compliance with approved norms, cultivating an atmosphere of fear and reprisal against those who speak out, lack of courage by leadership at all levels to speak up and correct deficiencies, and group think supporting non-standard methods and practices, all the while pinning the blame on those most junior and most vulnerable to wrongful influence and stifling. Take some fucking responsibility you Fucks!

Following his MISHAP a few months later his wife asked if I would be willing to provide any information I had regarding the circumstances surrounding his death and the MISHAP and more so just insight I might have into what was going on at the squadron. I told her everything that I have that would be helpful I'd be more than happy to share with her except that the information was tied up in an IG investigation that I believed would be fully investigated and results made public, and that it was pre-mature and inappropriate for me to discuss any specific details at that point. I simply told her that everything Wes had told her about what was going on was true. I told her later during this process, once it was clear a full investigation was not happening, that I still thought it was best for her efforts to remain independent from the result of my case and that I thought this approach would be best and simply reinforced the work she was trying to do by having two independent viewpoints reporting on similar if not the same situations and information. I don't know if that was the right decision or not, maybe I should have just stopped and turned everything I had over to her to include in her reporting. Regardless, she has her and Wes's work and I have mine and at least in my mind they both tell the same sad and heartbreaking story that was preventable, about human nature and leaders gone awry, and good people trying to do the right thing. I like to believe they are mutually supportive. She has surpassed any effort I've ever made on this subject and continues to do so; while I may have a choice to walk away from this any time I want, she never can, so this at least motivates me to keep trying to make a difference through the writing of all this. I hope this information helps her in some small way and provides added realization to her and Wes's extended family and friends that his efforts and reporting were all valid, he was spot on in his assessments, and as a result we lost a great leader along with other great leaders because leaders at all different levels in the chain became lost in the sauce of fear, politics, lack of moral courage, and greedy self-interest. I have no doubt many of them still are and probably in command today.

Chapter One—The Report

Period 1 Aug2010-April2011

Selection for DH

I found out in June July 2010 timeframe that I made operational department head while on IA (Individual Augmentee) assignment to Stuttgart Germany from USS Enterprise. That was an awesome experience by the way professionally and personally, and I was pleasantly surprised about the pick-up as stated before. I returned to Virginia in August, departed the Ship, and checked into the FRS to start my refresher training for the 53. Did I mention CAPT ******* was the Skipper on Enterprise when I checked out right before he was fired, interesting tidbit, I met him once shook his hand and saluted him as I departed the Ship.

AWSTS

I checked into Airborne Mine Countermeasures Weapons Systems Training School (AWSTS) in the fall 2010. There was nothing strange to report. I was excited to have the opportunity to fly the 53 again. The only thing I recall funny but didn't think anything of it at the time was when I walked across the street to check in with the HM-14 Skipper CDR ▮▮▮ he didn't even know I was going to be one of his department heads.

I do not think my performance in the aircraft was poor by any means but a final evaluation was made by the NATOPS instructor at the time LT ▮▮▮▮▮ directly to the XO at HM-14 CDR ▮▮▮ CDR D. It stated in an email that basically I met the minimum qualifications to be an aircraft commander (HAC) but that I should be identified as higher risk (something to that extent) but I was a HAC nonetheless. I only know about the nature of this email because CDR ▮▮▮ CDR D shared it with me, of course I didn't save a copy; why would I? I didn't mind the challenge that he was suggesting. I knew I was starting out as someone returning to the cockpit after a large break and that I had to be honest with myself about my

32

limitations. The reason for the email I found out later was due to a requirement stemming from an earlier

MISHAP where a returning DH with low flight hours, a long break in between, and a superiority complex

(overconfidence/invincibility) pushed a flight in bad and over challenging conditions and flew his crew

into a radio tower in TX killing everyone in his crew except for him. I learned that one of the

requirements following the accident was to flag potential returning department heads who might meet

this profile. I of course had low flight hours and a long break in between but I would definitely not

consider myself having any sort of a superiority complex. Or do I? I will say I'm confident in my

abilities and I think I am my toughest critic but I think I was indirectly and wrongfully labeled early on

which gave some of my opponents fuel to say that I was uncomfortable or scared in the aircraft because I

was cautious and alternatively did not like to push bad situations. I don't mind the challenge and don't

fault anyone for being a confident A-type personality since this is what you find in any squadron

(relentless challenging of each other's abilities) but I found what started as a cautionary tale of best safety

practice morphed into something much more targeted and slanderous that would be used against me in

the end.

Safety School

  To put it simply, my classmate ████████ was initially asked to be Safety Officer when we

checked in to HM-14. I was supposed to be Admin Officer. ██ didn't want to be Safety Officer and

said he was taking Admin so I volun-told took Safety. I say this and it sounds somewhat like I was

frustrated or disappointed but I wasn't. Actually, I didn't mind it and was looking forward to the job,

didn't really matter what job it was even though you really only had three choices starting out as the new

department head, Admin, Safety, or MCM Maintenance Officer. I looked forward to the academics of

Safety School not to mention safety school is a month long down in Pensacola. Aviation Safety Officer

(ASO) School I thought was pretty exciting because you get the chance to analyze the parts and pieces of

the tragedy in a way that you wouldn't normally get to or want to see it, try and understand it, and then

reproduce the scene in order to understand what caused it and prevent whatever led to the MISHAP from

happening in the future. Breaking it down and putting it back together again and learning from the

process is kind of

the idea. When I was at the school I remember thinking that I was stepping into a challenging safety

environment because I remember the attitude towards the safety program before when I was there as a JO.

I knew there would be resistance to any change of any sort particularly squadron established norms set by

the other department heads, XO and CO but I didn't realize just how pervasive the resistance would be

nor the immediate dangers being created by the non-standard practices being carried out and directed or

turned a blind eye by leadership. The senior department heads when I checked in referred to themselves

as the "brain trust," whatever the hell that means. Maybe that's why I'm where I am today, that I just

didn't get it. I always remembered as a JO on my first tour hearing the reference by many that you just

need to drink the Kool-Aid otherwise you just won't fit in and will always face resistance as an outsider.

When I was at Safety School I didn't plan for any of this to happen but I did approach the school in a way

that prepared me for a great challenge ahead to build legitimacy for a program that really had very little

say or influence over what was going on in the squadron. I saw and knew the work of previous safety

officers, what they went through, and people's attitudes towards them. To prevent getting more

philosophical, I planned on doing a good job and making a difference. Not knowing exactly what this

entailed, during the practical final exercise you had to develop a 30 60 90 schedule and routine for what

you intended to accomplish, some things pre-determined based on policy and instruction and others just

having to do with communicating about the details of the program and safety awareness. In a very rough

draft sort of way this is the first time I envisioned some sort of monthly safety report that attempted to

capture an ongoing timeline and accounting of safety information about where you've been, where you

are, and where this information is telling you to go to stay ahead of the power curve. This would be I

suppose the only way to disrupt the elements of the Swiss cheese as early as possible by being aware and

see them, identify them when they are coming together in a catastrophic way. The most memorable guest

speaker was a former Marine pilot who had gotten out and joined the Coast Guard. He basically

described a toxic safety and command environment that he knew would foster conditions for and

eventually lead to a severe MISHAP. He tried to speak out and control as much as he could through his

efforts as Safety Officer and the elements of the safety program but eventually he found himself constantly at odds with his CO and unable to prevent the toxic behaviors and attitudes from prevailing. I

graduated, got my certificate and left. His presentation was merely a warning to the group of the worst

possible case that you could find yourself in as Safety Officer. I didn't realize at the time the Hell he was

describing was speaking directly to me.

Check in

Check-in to HM-14 a second time was uneventful. I honestly can't remember if I checked in

before or after I went to Safety School. I think it was before simply because I think the squadron had to

pay for it and therefore they needed to officially own me on the books before sending me. I don't recall

getting any passdown. I began slowly picking up the pieces of a program in complete disrepair as I saw it

and used my 30 60 90 schedule as a guide. I was also flying again which was awesome. I had a lot to

look forward to. I had no reason to believe there was anything strange going on or would be going on

with regard to me and my progression in the squadron. I got along well with the other department heads,

aircrew, senior enlisted and I thought starting out my relationship with the CO CDR D ███ and XO CDR A ███ was

pretty good. I even remember doing some back in the saddle flights with CDR A ███ early on. I did sense

very early on a sort of funk in the overarching atmosphere of the squadron, a sort of ground hog day due

to the vicious cycle of being forced to do more with less, not enough qualified maintainers, not enough

time to get everything done, not enough people let alone qualified people, not enough parts for aircraft,

and in general just not a good understanding of a workable schedule that connected everybody's day to

day activities with a solid goal for the future and vision of any leadership that could describe the path to

get there. Very much was there a sense that beatings would continue until morale improved. This was

the first time I started thinking about culture and command climate as a safety issue that needed some

attention but I knew even back then that it wasn't a good idea to tell the squadron particularly the CO that

life at the squadron sucks and we need to do something about it. On the surface people smiled and said

sir and ma'am and work progressed but there was something underlying that I couldn't put my finger on

yet. I came up with an idea that I thought would be an acceptable way to engage the problem and begin to fix it. The 5050 draft was basically like a team building sports day where we set work aside for a day and just enjoy blowing off some steam. Can't remember exactly what I called the event but I remember approaching the "brain trust" about it and basically was met with two things—this is a stupid idea, and are you suggesting there's something wrong inside the squadron? I couldn't really push back on either yet because what was I basing my feelings and instincts on? I was basically changing and instating new policy to make a correction to something that I couldn't identify yet without more of an argument to support it. So I went on about my business and it didn't go any farther than that.

Period 2 April2011-Nov2011

Pen FOD

Sometime that Summer I went out to preflight the FCF. I don't remember exactly who my co-pilot was but perhaps ████████████. Ah hell I don't even remember if I was the HAC. I must be getting old. What I remember was the first time I witnessed something terribly wrong within the leadership and make-up and inner workings of the squadron. I felt very quickly that I knew from that point forward that there was something seriously wrong and that whether the other people around the room could see it or not I knew I had to make a more concerted effort to investigate what in the Hell was really going on.

When I checked the starboard e-bay compartment on preflight I found a standard government pen resting up on a shelf next to one of the control rod bell cranks. This is bad for several reasons but in terms of flying any FOD is bad and made even worse in the vicinity of the flight controls because they could potential cause binding and a restriction in the flight controls. The other primary reason this was bad is because the pen's location could not have happened by accident, somebody would have had to place it there. So it wasn't just that somebody dropped or forgot their pen on the aircraft and it fell into a crevice or they placed it somewhere in the aircraft on accident and forgot it haphazardly. Not only was this pen placed there but it was placed there with an intent to do harm or at least send a message and get people's attention. Now I know this is a lofty charge without more evidence but from a safety perspective this was no accident and required more of an explanation. I took a picture with my iPhone and took the issue straight to the XO [CDR A ████]. After reviewing the picture he called up the MO ████. I explained that before I would accept the aircraft (I guess I was the FCP) I wanted a full head to tail FOD inspection completed. ████ was not happy about this and basically shrugged off finding FOD on the aircraft as commonplace and he wasn't going to let some potential stunt by somebody create unnecessary burden on the overstressed maintenance team just because somebody was trying to get some attention. Apparently not long before that the command had some charges investigated for suspected sabotage. So the MO's stance was this was no big deal, we've already dealt with these things and it's a waste of time to waste more time looking into and giving the alleged the satisfaction of creating havoc in the maintenance department. The XO agreed with the MO and told me that he wanted someone else to take the aircraft because he thought I was visibly scared but that he thought the aircraft was acceptable to go FCF without further investigation into how or why that pen was there. I was not happy about this decision but at that time I was accepting of the decision and went about my day. This whole situation that just transpired indicated many things to me that I was going to start piecing together little by little. Either the maintenance department and leadership were being blind to the obvious cries for help or were aware of the dysfunction and choosing not to change anything or speak up. This also told me that safety concerns and even more so the Safety Officer had very little influence over the inner workings of the day to day operations on the ground or up in the air. It also indicated to me that if the XO and CO were not aware of why this was such a large problem then I needed to start presenting the case more clearly to them through a continuous reporting process to drive it home. The interaction of the XO taking me off the flight also caused me concern not really knowing how personal a decision this was towards me or professionally to make me learn my place or some other reason maybe because he was afraid I'd make more waves by being kept on the flight. When I asked other maintenance leadership at the senior enlisted and LPO level about the pen and how it got there the explanations were also indicative of something concerning because they were so obviously wrong and absent of any common sense or desire for truth and devoid of reason.

The two explanations I remember were that somebody sitting in the cockpit dropped a pen and it fell into that position from inside the cockpit. This is outrageous because that is not physically possible. The other explanation was that somebody for training purposes possibly an aircrewman placed the pen there and forgot it. This was my first insight that something below the top leadership level was also not right. My criticism in this manner isn't meant to describe these individuals as stupid but to suggest that because the responses were so ridiculous I thought it could only be meant as an indirect suggestion that "yes" they knew this was stupid and outrageous and that I'd be stupid to not think something was seriously wrong behind the scenes. Almost as though they were indirectly trying to communicate to me about something that they couldn't just come forward and say. Kind of like, "I know I'm part of this train that is heading down the tracks toward something bad but I can't do anything to stop it but I can at least acknowledge the absurdity of it and hope someone else listening can do something; if I say anything they'll just kick me off the train and it will keep on going." Almost a sense of helplessness to the point of hopelessness.

Hurrex

That summer I began to implement some type of consolidated safety reporting approach which would become the monthly safety reports. I gave the leadership the benefit of the doubt that up to that point they just maybe weren't getting the full picture and understanding of what was going on because for some reason the safety program had been allowed to fall silent into the crevices of the walls and passageways, always there watching as if only as a whisper in the conscience of everybody's minds. Leadership and everybody in the squadron had to know they were all accountable for a safety program right? I really don't know what they knew and didn't know at that point but what I did know is that there was a story that needed to get unraveled and told to the CO and XO as to the safety health of the squadron and I was determined to tell it well, simply, because that was my job. I knew that in order to tell the story and have it not be completely subjective, "sir/ma'am, this is what I think is going on," I would need to begin looking at the problem through the lens of as many independent markers and indicators as possible to connect the dots and form a picture a more complete understanding of what was going on and why.

The analysis could not simply be based on subjective measures; I needed to be able to collect data that was empirical and objective to tell the story and apply some kind of measured understanding of how bad things really were and how these incidents and behaviors I was tracking was going to eventually lead to unintended but preventable tragedy if we just recognized the danger and made small course corrections. If they started to corroborate the same data point then I could quantitatively and verifiably say that a trend of some kind was forming. One of these independent reporting mechanisms was through the HAZREP program. Interestingly enough, HAZREPS represent a key understanding as to the safety awareness and health of the squadron. First because it requires individuals to report any incident where something occurs that could have led to a MISHAP but didn't or simply didn't meet the threshold numbers for a MISHAP report. This reporting requirement is pretty broad and can interpreted many different ways by leadership as to what they are required to report. Some people are wary of reporting on everything because it can begin to raise doubt about a specific leader's performance. Others may feel that more reporting makes them appear more safety conscious and if in the right leadership atmosphere that is a good thing. So getting people to report errors on themselves essentially is the first step. The second step is to leverage the process to learn from and communicate mistakes to prevent a repeat and help others avoid similar mistakes in their squadrons. I came to find that not only were we stuck in an atmosphere of not reporting but that there was resistance to report and only report when absolutely necessary, only doing so in a way that didn't allow too much light to extend behind the curtain. There were also institutional layers to consider that caused resistance too. Even when leadership may want to support a strong reporting program, leadership is always dependent on the people doing the work and the programs that govern the work getting done to be accountable and tell on themselves when something occurs. So I started listening to the whispers and subtle things going on around the squadron that maybe people were trying to communicate or that simply people were ignoring. I started pushing to report HAZREPS. Immediately incidents started to float to the surface and it didn't take long once the questions started that there was more and more to the story to tell and that led to more to report and that led to a pretty solid picture of human factors errors running rampant at all levels of the squadron from the maintenance department to the front office to the culture in operations. Everybody knew things were bad, things were getting done improperly, leadership was silently complicit-openly ignored-or directly involved in some cases, people were open behind closed doors but out in the open nobody wanted to say nothin'. As I started to see this story unfolding and I began trying to paint the picture for leadership on a silver platter through the monthly safety reports I was also beginning to see my own personal dynamics with leadership begin to unravel at the seams. Culminating early during a blowup in the XO's office, I threw my wings on his desk and accused him of lying to my face telling him I didn't want to have any part of this and left. Sometimes I think I could've handled this differently but now looking back I regret nothing and stick by my decision essentially telling him to fuck off; I should've used those exact words. I still think he was a liar then and continues to be a liar to this day for his denial of his part in my inquiry and reprisal against me. Fuck you dude! Nonetheless, the Skipper let me continue and I had to eat some crow if I wanted to stay on the team. I reached out to an old friend who told me that was the best course of action, apologize and move on regardless of the outcome. Long story short, I could no longer separate what I was finding on the ground with what we were asking people to do up in the air and how we were conducting ourselves operationally. This really bothered me though as you could tell from my write-up and I struggled from that point on to really gain favor with anybody particularly the leadership. I had given them ammunition to use against me but I still didn't fully understand the gravity of everything that was going on. I just knew I found myself in a very dysfunctional command environment that was becoming more and more hostile towards me and how I was reporting key safety aspects of my work.

Human Factors Board (HFB) #1

As a result of my unruly behavior (forget the behavior of others mind you) I was awarded with an extremely informal even inappropriate Human Factors Board (HFB) in the CO's office. Still to this day I don't understand its purpose other than to attempt to formally document in their minds what had transpired but do so in a way that placed all the responsibility on my shoulders as a bad actor and troublemaker. I did my best to play the game and go along with it just to move on but I knew it was wrong on so many levels and so did everybody else. My aggressively speaking out at that point had not really achieved the point in which I'd hoped it would so I returned to flying and my monthly safety reports and turned up the heat. There was either something wrong with me or something wrong with the system I was in and the people driving it. Deep down I knew it wasn't me, but you get enough people saying something and it can be hard not to start to believe them. Sometimes even my wife took their side and was just telling me to shut up and stop making waves. This was uncomfortable, it's always uncomfortable when you start finding yourself on the outside of the team. The military system is not designed that way, people are brought up and raised to gravitate towards uniformity and conformity so if you find yourself having to shake the bushes it's probably not a good thing. This began a very stressful period but I tried to remain as objective as possible and focus on the job.

VulcanEx 12-1

I'm not afraid of my government. I believe in its institutions. I think in this case its institutions simply failed. For this segment I find myself at sort of a crossroads. I've been given a leadership opportunity despite being taken off the Korea DET OIC rotation. I found out second hand about that change while flying with the person that replaced me in casual conversation in the cockpit during a night familiarization (FAM) when he told me that he was getting ready to go to Korea to take over as OIC. I said that that was funny because I was supposed to be going during that same time. The normal on-track rotation as a department head was to spend a few months in your first job, do a small DET OIC for a HARP or other exercise, and then deploy as OIC for six months, return as OPSO or MO and then move on. That was the first I was hearing there was a change in the plan. Since that spring when I checked-in I was scheduled to be the OIC for VulcanEx and then deploy to Korea not long after. And then during that night flight I heard I was being taken off the rotation indefinitely. I confronted the XO and you know how that conversation went. Bottom line is, as mentioned before, I accused him of lying to me and I turned in my wings on his desk and told him that I didn't want to be a part of whatever this was that was going on anymore. I said I thought it was shady underhanded and simply not right. There followed many manipulations to my career progression in the squadron which CO's do have some right to and control over but there are limits to what they can do to you and how they get to run you out. This was an early indication that I didn't appreciate at the time of how the CO would shape his authority around controlling what he would do with me professionally in the squadron, and I did not handle it well. Some people might say in hindsight the best thing to do is shut the fuck up, which was the prevailing approach by everybody. The problem then is that I knew the issues before me would simply continue putting people and the aircraft at unnecessary risk. So was I just a scapegoat then and he was smart enough to have that be the plan from the beginning that I would do all this great work, pin it on me as the unstable one, and walk away from the crimescene? Was there any way in hindsight for me to do the right thing in this case without being self-sacrificed? I would love to hear all the ways of what I should've done differently in order to expose the truth and keep my career. He succeeded in being able to separate what he was doing to me professionally with what he and others were getting away with illegally in directing the violation of safety/maintenance practices (either openly or by turning a blind eye) and his illegal retaliation against me for the efforts I made as Safety Officer to report it and expose not just what was going on but leadership's culpability in it and the subsequent unfair personnel actions. He either succeeded in this endeavor or the IG gave him a pass and allowed him to get away with it, and the Navy, and DoD, and the Congressional Office, and the others who chose not to speak out and get behind me when the opportunity presented itself. They are all now culpable. After being given an opportunity to think about my decision to turn in my wings by the CO I rescinded my decision after consulting some old friends and stuck it out. I received a normal FITREP at that point and then took the detachment down to Panama City to try and tackle the HARP (Helicopter Advanced Readiness Program) Exercise. We called it VulcanEx, our sister squadron called it HawkEx because our callsigns were Vulcan and Blackhawk respectively. I'd been battling these suspected maintenance woes trying to better understand and shed light onto what was going on as the underlying problems. I was faced with a reversal to this problem because I was now going to be in charge of the aircraft, people, and the process behind keeping everything going under the pressure and scrutiny of a simulated battle problem. At the end of the day we did pretty good. You can see the after action report results for better clarification [2]. Despite these best efforts which I don't think you could have really done much better, the decision to keep me off the Korea DET OIC rotation would stand. I didn't really fix the maintenance process or change anything in the pubs. My approach was pretty simple, identify the problems as early as possible, get them fixed and then get back to flying. Not to get into too much detail but I studied previous VulcanEx results to better understand what the problems were. I had also been on many of them as a LT and knew from that perspective how they approached the problem which was to shove as much ten pounds of crap into a 5 pound sack with the aircraft. I thought that if the approach was proven to not be sustainable and not work then why did we keep doing it that way. I kept the flight schedule light, only two sorties per aircraft and extended each flight out to 4 hours so that morning weather and maintenance delays could still be absorbed and hopefully get at least a two plus hour flight completed. The goal was to get into a sustainable battle rhythm where the people and machines were all working in unison. We got into this rhythm earlier than expected and had some good luck with weather. As far as maintenance and their process was concerned, the only thing I instructed for them was to give them as much time as possible to get the aircraft fixed and turned around for the next day. In the past I observed OIC's trying to squeeze the turnip by flying aircraft using as much available light as possible to make up for previously lost events thinking that this would maximize efficiency, basically if you had opportunity then you had to utilize it. I decided to reduce the fly day and if there was any left over at the end I'd give it back to maintenance as early as possible to get the aircraft turned around and give the tactics folks as much time as possible to turn around their process. I believed that if we gave maintenance an opportunity to do things the right way with enough time then the proper results would follow. I also thought that if issues did arise I wanted them to be able to bring them to my attention as opposed to feeling like they needed to meet some fictitious sense of urgency that I was placing on them because of the exercise. Everybody did a great job, I claim very little except that I was the OIC, I had to make some tough decisions which people doubted and not everybody liked and in the end it worked and we were all successful. I simply tried to approach the leadership opportunity in a manner that would bring the best, not the worst, out in the people doing the hard work, I was simply the cruise director trying to make things run smoothly so the team could accomplish the mission. If you intentionally put people into impossible situations for the wrong reasons then I believe you will bring out the worst in them because they won't believe in you nor care about what they are doing and believe in themselves why they are doing it; the opposite of relying on each other as a team of professionals to persevere. We had some hiccups but for the most part I tried to show everybody mutual respect by working hard, trying to do the right thing, communicating clearly and openly, allow best practices to boil to the top, and keeping everybody engaged particularly myself and the chain of command.

At this point I would say that I started feeling like the guy in Matrix, who decided to take the pill that un-flushed his brain so he could see the world for what was actually happening around him. I should've swallowed the other pill I would sometimes think and just go back to dreaming everything was O.K. Even after having such a successful detachment under my belt I still apparently was not good enough or competitive enough to be tapped for greater responsibility over others in the squadron with far less tactical experience. The counter-narrative against me by the command (CO and others) in the end after all was said and done is that I was a struggling department head and pilot with low flight hours that was overcompensating for my weaknesses by over performing at my ground job, who lacked the leadership skills and tactical experience to handle being the OIC in Korea let alone one day a CO, who was emotionally unstable and couldn't handle the operational stress of flying and needed to be grounded, who required heavy supervision because of my frequent outbursts and inability to get along with others, and lastly who didn't have the mental toughness to do the job and required professional psychiatric help. The truth is that I'll own all of it, because even after you peel back everything none of that really matters if you want to believe any of what they said about me or not. So yes I did struggle, I was low flight time, I was at odds with many people I worked with, I was never in the running to be CO and probably wasn't the best candidate among others to be OIC, I did have outbursts on occasion when I got pissy, and I was emotional about what was going on around me, and I certainly needed help in many ways. To add to all this many might say that my extended family also suffers from mental illness and many are heavily medicated. I've been to counseling before in my lifetime and I think it can be incredibly useful under the

right circumstances. Now whether you want to believe I had the "right stuff" in the air and on the ground

as a leader and who possessed the mental toughness to do the job I must leave up to you and my critics to

decide. I'd say my record continues up to this point to speak for itself even after the scrutiny and turmoil

this whole situation has put me, my family, and my career through. In this process I simply did my best

to present and align my safety narrative with that of the front office as a consolidated and unified front to

properly reflect the reality of what was going on within the squadron and make the necessary changes to

fix problems. That was my job to represent the CO and make sure he/she had the best information

possible to make decisions. From the beginning I experienced pushback about my approach and what I

was saying and doing but still (to CDR D credit) was able to communicate rather openly to leadership

and push forward with the safety initiatives I was trying to implement. I guess the real turning point for

me became when I realized that my safety narrative started to diverge, taking on a different reality from

that of the CO even though seemingly was based on the same set of facts; this started happening directly

before and after when the MISHAPs began that Summer 2012 but was probably set into motion much

sooner than that when my relationship soured with the maintenance officer at the time. Of course

MISHAPS occurred despite my best efforts through the safety program and in the aftermath my belief

was that the truth had to be vigorously reported to make sure everybody was on the same page about what

had happened and why. I felt there were real problems before within the squadron's culture but it wasn't

until that transition through the MISHAPs period where I had clear indication that the leadership at the

very top was a direct part of the problem too; intentionally trying to sideline me, silence me, and discredit

me in a very systematic and deliberate manner. In addition, I could only conclude based on the facts I had

been assertively reporting and observing that concerted efforts were beginning to take shape to conceal

and disconnect the narrative with what was really going on in order to soften the blow and lessen the

scrutiny from higher perhaps, and avoid the true nature of the MISHAPs from being revealed, and

essentially cover people's asses. The other department heads and others in the squadron witnessed

everything that was going on, acknowledged as much to me in private, and stood by and did nothing. I was on my own…and nothing I could do in the squadron was going to change unless I pounded the drum even louder.

Period 3 Nov2011-April2012

Monthly Safety Reports

The monthly safety reports were my way of not only holding myself accountable and organized for what I was doing but also to communicate directly with the front office and convey the big picture of how I was putting into action the squadron's safety program. Ironically, I was re-building the safety program and writing the instruction at the same time while I was trying to implement it. I had lots of independent feelers out that I was tracking to help keep the safety pulse on what was going on around the squadron and what was connected and what wasn't. I found people were pretty open about coming forward in private and forthcoming most of the time if asked directly. The safety program also included a monthly safety newsletter that I would use to communicate safety issues and narratives directly with the squadron that I would hang in the heads (bathrooms) etc. I started sending out HAZREPS any opportunity I could based on the information I was uncovering, many of which would never have seen the light of day if I didn't push them.

AGB Driveshaft

Sometimes the incident was pretty damning but deserved recognition by the individual because truly a MISHAP had been averted. In this case, on the postflight inspection the maintainer found that a wire coated hydraulic hose had been installed in a manner that allowed it move loosely in the forward AGB compartment so that it was resting in place in contact with the AGB driveshaft. The result, following the previous flight and potentially other flights since the condition required pretty significant time to reach the severity of the damage, was that the driveshaft had been nearly worn through to the point of failure. These driveshafts are designed to fail at specific points in a specific manner. This failure would have been unique and occurred directly in the middle of the driveshaft probably on the next flight.

Losing the AGB as a result of the failure alone can be catastrophic due to the loss of critical equipment such as hydraulic boost but the second order effect is the material damage in the compartment due to the flying metal and debris at such a high RPM. The ramifications of this failure if not caught at this particular time would very likely have been catastrophic for the crew. It was a simple mistake of not tying off the hydraulic line properly to remain clear of the moving parts of the driveshaft. I did not receive pushback from sending the HAZREP. I took a picture of the maintainer who found it and attempted to recognize him in a maintenance and safety magazine to go on the cover of the publication with a short write up but it was not approved. I do not know at what level this was shot down but no other story of recognition was more deserving that month and the picture and story that was selected definitely wasn't as good. I could only assume there was an optics problem that forced somebody to pull it back or did the Skipper, I don't know. It represented exactly the type of story and important information you'd want published in an aviation maintenance safety magazine.

Korea DET

I mentioned before about the decision for me not be OIC in Korea. Early on they fed me a line by telling me that maybe I would be able to go later. By December it was clear they had no intention of sending me anywhere. I felt as though I was riding a fine line between trying to play the game to get along with everybody against doing my job which was to continue pounding the safety drums until leadership got their heads out of their asses. It was also time for me to take over as OPS or MO because my time as Safety Officer should've been up. I got the same response about the Korea DET which was that maybe I'd take over one of them later on but not now. It also became increasingly clear as I went on that there was nothing about my situation and time at the squadron that would improve my situation and be career enhancing. I was deliberately being sidelined the more I pushed and if I asked the question all I would get were excuses. Before turning in my wings I told the XO that not being the Korea DET OIC would take me out of competitive running within the squadron and essentially torpedo my career if I can't compete for a #1 or #2 EP leaving the squadron. The XO told me that my career would not be negatively impacted by these decisions being made to hold me back from OIC; a bold faced lie and I told him that (as mentioned before I threw my wings on his desk). On the surface it appeared though that my work in safety was all being appreciated until it wasn't. I started to find clear signs that the human factors problems that existed were not just some isolated incidents of young inexperienced Sailors making mistakes but that the squadron culture, maintenance programs, and leadership driving day to day operations were implicit, complicit, and sometimes directing malfeasance and actions known to be wrong. Personnel were acting fearful about speaking to me or giving me information. The next part is kind of poignant. As I pushed harder I had leadership within the maintenance department becoming combative, one instance ███ barged into my office and started berating me about the HAZREPS I'd been pushing. To me, this person is a dipshit. Another time ███ bucked up on me yelling out in the open in front of everybody that I tricked him when the safety inspection team arrived for a surprise look. I liked ███ but in that instance I thought he was a real dipshit too. Obviously you can see the email response from ██, he and I butted heads and I made how I felt about him pretty well known. I didn't have such an issue with him being a piece of shit, my issue was that he was a piece of shit who did shit in his personal life and then threatened the people around him to keep their mouth shut so ████████ wouldn't find out. Fuck you dude, make your own bed. Not to mention ███, fucker! Nonetheless, there were also the silent wait and see types like ███ and ██. ████ and ███ were both assholes too, couldn't tow worth a shit but had no problems moving up in the squadron. Other leadership outside the squadron too, ███ and █, all dipshits. I'm sure they are not singing my praises neither. Of course pretty much everybody involved got promoted and moved on so maybe I'm the dipshit. If you choose to speak out you must be prepared to own being the dipshit because that's what you are to them and that's O.K. The other department heads that I most aligned with I don't really know where they stood, they were all afraid. I made it pretty clear to them where I stood. Even ████ who I thought for sure would speak her mind if simply given the correct opportunity but in the end none of it seemed to matter and as far as I know they all kept their mouths shut. I'm where I am and they are where they are; I've had enough time to get over it even though probably appears I'm still pretty sore, I guess I am.

Twins

My wife and I welcomed twins to the world in Jan 2012. What a great experience. Not so from the perspective of the squadron. I started communicating to leadership, department head meetings, and making preparations early on around November about the uncertainty of the window when she might go into labor but that I had organized all the safety related activities in a manner that I could take my leave without impact. I also clearly communicated the amount of time I intended to take as I was saving up my leave. So I thought I had squared everything away very effectively until three days after the birth when I got a phone call from the XO questioning where I was and the amount of leave I had submitted; when he asked me where I was I told him I was at the hospital (or possibly at home at that point I think); he thought it was too much leave. Man was my wife pissed, of course she messaged the CO's wife and for one reason or another the CO told him to back-off. I'm glad he did because my wife was about to kick my ass and I was about to kick the XO's ass. Mind you they were never intending to send me anywhere for deployment any time soon. I once thought in November that maybe there was still a chance but by the time January rolled around it was clear to me. I couldn't do anything about the squadron not having their shit together but I had my shit together so I was going to be gone for three weeks of combined leave and no one was going to miss me at work. I was also having twins so if you're not going to deploy me or let me advance in the squadron what did you think I was going to do. So what was the fucking problem assholes? Let me fucking be! Of course I was more cordial about my interactions at the time but what a shit-show. Ironically, or maybe not ironically, military is now allowed to take up to 3 weeks mandatory baby leave. Fuck you CDR A█████, dipshit!

Period 4 April2012-August2012

Safety Center Rep Documentation

I was in contact with the Naval Safety Center down the street early on for obvious reasons initially for the HAZREPS and setting up inspections. CDR █████████ was over there at the time and he initially helped out with if I remember correctly during our first safety stand down to present a discussion about human factors and how they relate to MISHAPS. At some point upon reaching out to him for advice on some of the issues I was dealing with I specifically remember him telling me, "document everything." As though he recognized exactly where things were going and that was the best advice he could give me. ██████ gave me the feedback on the CAD firing HAZREP which ██████ became so up in arms with me about. If I recall he was also in Korea with us as the Safety Center rep. He was the only person I came across who was truly helpful in trying to navigate the issues I was facing with the squadron and its safety program and leadership. Despite his best efforts I think he got to the point where he was muffled too once telling me that at the end of the day the CO is still the CO and that basically there was nothing he could do.

Inspections

The reality of MISHAPS occurring became more of an issue of "when" not "if." I tried to set up as many preventative measures as possible to try and stop any holes I could from aligning. We had gotten extremely lucky on several occasions already especially with the AGB driveshaft and that was just with the incidents that we knew about or had been reported. The wildcard which I completely neglected and had no SA on until later was with the Korea DET; I had no idea what was going on out there or how bad things were, I really was only able to see into the squadron's health at home and I had no access to be able to see anything without actually being out there. It did cross my mind later that perhaps there was more to the reason why they didn't allow me to go out there to be OIC, not just because I wasn't a qualified competitive candidate which they were claiming.

When the safety inspection team came in I couldn't be more relieved. I thought for sure this was all I needed to do to blow the lid on what was going on but surprisingly they came and went with no report, at least that I had access to. I was even more frustrated, "what the hell was going on?" I would think to myself. At some point you have to start questioning the validity of what you're doing because you know in the back of your head the path it's taking you down when you go head to head with leadership in a military setting. You either have to shut up or be prepared to go all the way. Hell even my wife was questioning what I was doing and questioning that maybe I was the one that was screwed up and why was I making so many waves not getting along with everybody. I stood by my analysis though and I knew the data I had been gathering was valid and was leading down the correct path of understanding. I started to reveal that the reason leadership didn't like it was because the conclusion I was reaching was that they were all complicit and essentially behind the steering wheel. I think they the leadership would say that I was simply doing exactly what they had directed me to do, and that they were aware of the situation and taking appropriate action to mitigate what was going on, and that their support for all my safety efforts was a clear indication of their support for me and the safety program. Well they're full of shit because pretty much the whole time the only reason I was able to convince anybody to do anything on the safety schedule was because it was a documented requirement from higher. One small problem though, I guess they simply disagreed with me on the characterization of the causal factors behind what was going on, being linked directly back to a series of human factors and related to a culture being driven by the front office and supported by the community. Now you see this gets into some pretty squishy areas that I'll never be able to fully prove and at some point it becomes their words against mine. You figure if you bark up the chain loud enough and everybody still disagrees with you then you MUST be wrong. Well, I stick by my case and the evidence that supports it and whether preponderance of the evidence or beyond a reasonable doubt I think my story exceeds both thresholds to force someone to at least consider the alternative that maybe I'm not the crazy one here.

MISHAPS

What about the MISHAPS? There were several things going on all at once around the late spring time period. I'd returned from baby leave, flying was good, I'd had an extremely successful detachment to Panama City, I was still butting heads with the command but still I continued implementing the elements of the safety program I'd been working to establish and stick to the timeline of events as best I could to raise awareness and try to break up the Swiss cheese and get as many risk mitigations in place as possible to thwart catastrophe. At that point I had clearly come to odds with the maintenance department leadership primarily the MO and the QA division was stuck in the middle between my investigating and reporting against the reality they faced which was to basically continue doing things the same way they'd been doing even though I believe most if not all of them knew it was the wrong way of doing business. It seemed a battle was underway to balance established norms and standards against published manuals and instructions. Up until that point I'd really only focused on Homeguard and didn't have the bandwidth or reason to do much to look into the health of the detachment in Korea. They were always kind of off on their own, separate and independent, with a JO designated as the safety officer which I didn't really have much involvement with except to communicate with them before deploying. I don't remember exactly how I was notified about the first incident but I recall that it wasn't voluntarily by the normal methods, basically I found out by accident (as I did many other times) and as far as I could tell from the beginning nobody really intended to bring me into the loop. I'm pretty sure I found out in a side conversation with one of the junior enlisted who had mentioned it to me in casual conversation acting like I should've already known. I don't know if the mention was accidental or intentional but regardless I started asking questions and looking into it. As I peeled back the onion with more and more questions throughout the following days I realized there was a concerted effort to conceal the details of the initial investigation from me as I knew that at least a HAZREP needed to be sent. There was every effort, as was the norm, to try and interpret the instructions in a way to avoid having to send a report or tell anybody outside the command, just keep it internal, it was no big deal. Basically the OIC straight up told me no, that he wasn't going to provide me with the paperwork of the internal investigation. I went to the CO and explained the situation and demanded that I be provided the detachment's information about the incident. It took approval from the CO telling the OIC to send me the information before I got access to it. You can read the results about that incident separate. The next incident not long after had to do with destruction of an engine by a sprayer nozzle that had accidentally been shot into the intake during cleaning. And then soon after that we had our class alpha where the crew had to do an emergency landing in a farmer's field due to catching fire inflight in which the entire aircraft burned to the ground without anybody getting injured. I traveled out to conduct the MISHAP investigation and ██joined us I believe as the safety center representative. The long and short of all of it was, as the information came in and became more clear at least to me, that here was a story being told and underway about all the things I'd been reporting on all along for the past year regarding leadership awareness about what was going on, being openly and silently complicit and in some cases directing malpractice, people being afraid to speak up, leadership and Sailors not making required reports for safety and maintenance incidents, not following published procedure, a mentality that anything goes to get the mission done at any cost, an atmosphere of fear and intimidation retaliation against anybody who tries to speak out or fix things. The anomaly was a JO named Wes Vandorn. Wes was a good friend who was fun to fly with and work with as he was always challenging himself to understand the problem, fix it, and do things better. He was instrumental as the tactics officer in the success of the detachment I led in November. He only worked for me directly that one time. The rest of the time he spent in tactics and then got into maintenance as a division officer. I only recall him being out on DET for a short time before the MISHAP. He was an anomaly to this situation because although during the interviews most people were suddenly very open about the atmosphere and situation of what was actually going on he was the only one who was actively engaged in trying to change anything. He had been unsuccessful at simply being able to direct change so he spent a lot of time actually helping observe and assist the maintenance crews while they were conducting the maintenance and making sure things were being done by the book and trying to understand in some cases why things couldn't be or weren't being done by the book. In any case, the rest of the leadership were simply rubber stamps simply standing by letting things happen particularly the OIC who was suddenly very remorseful and open about things after the incidents started happening. I still think they should've fired his ass but instead they promoted him go figure. You can read about it in detail in the report but basically in addition to my safety story coming true in dramatic fashion, I couldn't convince anybody particularly the safety inspection team (aside from ████) that any of it was connected to what I'd been observing at Homeguard and that none of the human factors connections would be included in the report.

My last ditch effort was simply have it added as a causal factor we considered but was not causal to the MISHAPs. There was clear direction from higher I discovered that none of it would be included. How do I know this for certain? I don't, but I'm willing to make this assertion because I know for a fact that if you asked the other members they'd confirm it since I know the two sides (Skipper, XO, and senior member) were talking about the process. In fact I'm certain that if you asked the other department heads as to the validity of my reporting in hindsight they'd agree with me about what happened. Of course if that's the case why didn't the IG investigate the report? Good question—the reason is that people lied about the true nature of what was going on with the investigators or if they did tell the truth then the IG chose to not do the right thing. Either way the reporting was true and accurate, the information was intentionally withheld from the MISHAP reports to cover up reality, when I barked hemmed and hawed about what we were doing and how we were handling things I got sidelined reprimanded and slandered, and when I fought it over the past nearly 8 years I was told to shut the fuck up…yeah I'm pissed now! It's funny watching the news with all the impeachment trial back and forth because at the end of the day I'll be very surprised if the republican side bends on their votes or decides to call witness, not sure if Dems would do anything different if the tables were turned. I see many similarities at the top levels of government where the system intentionally resists allowing the right things to be done and be brought forward not just in terms of singular decisions but more so in collective decisions, group think, fear to speak out from the norm or prevailing opinion of the group. What are the reasons why people individually are kept from doing the right thing even when they clearly recognize what they need to do, and what are those things from the group that influence the individual in such a profound way to force them into an environment of fear and inaction against what clearly are acts of wrong doing after the fact? Case extended, why on earth are people so wrongly influenced all the time from being able to take corrective actions before-hand to prevent calamity they can clearly see on the horizon, maybe it's just that humans are instinctively self-destructive combined with an incessant self-preservation instinct with a need and desire to maintain control through the collective protection in numbers. Who the hell knows…so as I continue to observe the big picture I can't really be surprised any more that things turned out the way they did with decisions about my case turning out the way they did. The system has to protect itself and a decision to support me meant a decision against the institutions designed to keep the Navy and government going in the first place, people are too comfortable just keeping things the way they've always been for better or worse. That doesn't make it right and I don't have to be happy about it though. As I don't believe my story or case will change anything about the outcome I experienced but maybe people can be more aware about how they should handle their own similar sticky challenges especially in government. First, don't rock the boat, do whatever the boss tells you regardless of whether it's illegal or immoral. Second, follow any and all prevailing opinions and standards, if the group thinks it and follows it then it's the law and don't question it even if illegal or immoral. Three, if you see something wrong then simply look the other way and pretend you didn't see anything especially if illegal or immoral. Four, if you're in a leadership position and you find yourself with somebody like me who is clearly rocking the boat, slander the hell out of that person and destroy them characteristically because you have the upper hand and the institution will support you no matter what as long as their challenge against you is attacking the institutions that you represent…your good. Five, if you want to think for yourself, do it on your own time, and don't try and do the right thing even when it clearly presents itself because chances are you will be destroyed as a result and will not actually lead to any demonstrable change in the system causing the error. Oh and I forgot to mention that if you happen to think there is an institution or office that is designed and supposed to be there to protect you as you attempt to do the right thing and protect yourself against wrongdoing, well then you're wrong and you should go ahead and stab yourself in the back because they'll be standing by with the knife. At the end of the day I still don't believe any of this advice but unfortunately my own experiences cannot discount any of it from being true so you will have to decide what I should've done differently to save people from dying unnecessarily and prevent a failed system of leadership and individual personalities from killing them. War is supposed to be fought on the battlefield but more and more we see it taking place voluntarily in our own home; don't stand by and allow it. Do the right thing for Fucks Sake!

Aftermath

So what happened after the MISHAPs? I returned after two weeks in Korea investigating the MISHAP. Even though I included all the interviews and evidence into the reporting system with the report, the report itself did not reflect the true nature of what was really going on within the squadron in terms of the negative culture, atmosphere of fear and reprisal, hostile work environment, malpractice from taking place and being directed, and simply the failures in leadership. The safety center through ██ (who agreed with all my assessments because he'd been involved since the beginning almost) also did nothing to intervene. The safety center had conducted a safety inspection of the squadron and reported it to the CO but I'd been abruptly fired from Safety so I actually did not get to listen to the results. As far as I could tell the Skipper had been given a clean bill of health. He appeared to go into protection mode because not long after that I was presented with a non-punitive letter of caution stating that I was emotionally unstable and not safe to fly and that people didn't feel safe flying with me and that many people had issued concerns about me in the aircraft. I immediately was taken off the flight schedule and issued another human factors board. At the human factors board I was told by the Flight Doc that if I didn't submit myself to counseling then the CO was going to direct a psychological evaluation on me. Even though four sessions of counseling at Portsmouth determined I was fit for full duty the CO still punished me under this false pretense issuing a formal counseling sheet against me (apparently he would just hold onto for his safe keeping) that I would be allowed to fly again under strict scrutiny of the schedulers (who with and when) and dependent on whether I demonstrated any more emotional outbursts or any other reason the CO deemed appropriate or inappropriate, and that if I violated the terms then the CO would issue me for FNAEB/psychological evaluation. When all this started happening the whole thing felt like I was truly in the twilight zone. I went from reporting these issues to being the one that was being reported on, what a clever role reversal by the CO, congrats. And what could I do in my position, I felt pretty helpless at that point, people were talking and looking at me differently, pretty uncomfortable and undesirable position to be in. I felt like a pretty big example being made of around the squadron, "look at what happens to somebody that aggressively speaks out about what's going on particularly if it's against leadership." As I continued to fight and represent what was truly going on I found myself walking a fine line, sometimes doubting what I was doing and why I was doing it. Maybe I was the crazy one, maybe I should stop fighting, maybe everything that was being said about me was true, maybe I was crazy and I should just drink the Kool Aid, shut up and stop fighting to expose the truth. The other department heads and others in the squadron watched my demise and in private agreed with me about what was going on but nobody would speak out. The next thing I noticed I was presented by the NATOPS officer with an end of fiscal year flight time waiver to sign since I didn't meet my night time flying mins. I noticed that something different about mine that nobody else's had which was that in my characterization it mentioned that the requirement for the waiver was due to human factors related issues in addition to the normal reason being that we just didn't have enough flight time to go around to everybody. This was not necessary to put this in there and directly attacked my competence as a pilot because it made my alleged personal issues or human factors as being one of the reasons I wasn't getting my job done in the air. Basically telling the reader that I was fucked up in some way. I took it back to the NATOPS officer and was notified that if I didn't sign it "as is" then the CO was going to issue me for a FNAEB/psych evaluation. This was starting to become a common theme apparently. I took it to the Wing Safety officer to try and protest but the direction that he advised me on was to simply sign it and that the juice wasn't worth the squeeze basically to fight it. Ironically, it was this one piece of information in my initial complaint that the IG punted on and didn't issue any determination on as part of the unfair personnel actions against me. It wasn't that the IG considered it and didn't weigh in on a judgement, the IG simply didn't include it in the report at all by not recognizing it. I found it interesting that if they had included it and certainly considered it as an unfair personnel action then the date would have had it fall within the 60 day reporting requirement for when I submitted my complaint…hmmm—fuckers. It was around this time I started thinking about what the hell I was going to do in my position, fuck I got myself into this mess because I was doing a job that simply nobody else was willing to do and doing it in a way that needed to be done and now I was being overtly punished for how I had done it and a good job at it I might add. I went over to NCIS and talked to one of the agents about my situation and discussed wanting to issue a complaint or some kind of charge against what I felt was being done to me. Special Agent 6 ▓ (I believe was the nickname) advised that the issue sounded more like something for the IG to take

up. First I went over and had a sit down with an IG I believe it was in the old SURFLANT bldg now

SUBLANT and they advised if I wanted to continue then I should probably talk to the AIRLANT IG, Mr. 5 ▓. I finally made it over to Mr. 5 ▓ sometime I think around mid-Sep (I'd have to go back and check

my report) and told him my whole story that I'd told so many times in my reporting up the chain, to the

Portsmouth counselors, to the human factors board, to NCIS, and that I wanted now to file a formal

complaint and that I believed there would be an effort to further directly tarnish my record in my next

FITREP which was due at the end of October. **Mr. 5** advised me that I should go back and

organize all my materials for the complaint and wait until I receive my FITREP and then include it in

my formal complaint. (I fell for this trick hook line and sinker) What I should've done is sign the

paperwork right there and give the rest of the documents supporting later as I got them organized. I

went back and got everything together and wrote up my complaint and tried to tell the story as best I

could. October 31 came and went and so did my FITREP debrief; where was it? I didn't receive my

FITREP for whatever clever reason until the end of November. I shortly thereafter submitted my

complaint to **Mr. 5** at AIRLANT and didn't hear anything else about the final results until nearly

3.5 years later.

I'm tired of carrying this burden around with me. I think I'll stop there. I think I've said

everything I want to say. Sorry Nicole I wish I could've been stronger. I don't know what else I can do.

Public, do with this what you want.

I will say one last thing that our country is great because I have the opportunity to speak and tell

my story regardless of whether anyone is going to listen or agree with me or not. I hope some personal or

collective value of some kind will come to someone or situation as a result of this story and the

information provided in it.

Chapter Two—Search For Wholeness

Period 5 Aug2012-May2013

Protected Communications

Here I am again nearly eight years later sitting at my computer trying to recall and figure out what to do with this information. USNI told me I had to reach at least 100,000 words in order to be considered for publication so I guess I have to continue writing. I'm hoping that the forward will consist of written accounts from Nicole and others to officially capture their perspective and reveal a broader understanding and window into the human cost when supposedly good leaders choose to go along with or do bad things.

When I started being attacked in such an open and flagrant manner through these administrative fire bombs against me only one conclusion was clear. That was, they wanted me to shut the hell up, conceal what I was making an effort to say, and to shut me up they were going to squeeze me and discredit me and my character so that there could be just enough doubt into the validity of what I was saying or would say. I remember the CO's comment to me after my last monthly safety report submission and turnover report which was that if I intended to request an IG inspection I wouldn't be doing it as Safety Officer. At that point when I wrote it I thought I'd be consulting the IG to help us through an independent lens right the ship because we lacked the ability to see through our own ignorance and the walls we'd built within the community to protect and shield us from believing or seeing that anything we as a group were doing was wrong…I'm pretty sure this has been studied as group think. Other reports later showed this group think extended well beyond the walls of the squadron. Instead I found myself consulting the IG for protection. I'd been wronged professionally and the full story behind the safety, leadership, and MISHAP chaos was allowed to be kept under wraps in the usual manner, make those opposed simply go away.

Unfair Personnel Actions

I think I reported just a handful of Unfair Personnel Actions against me as a result of the protected communications I had made and was continuing to try and make. I think the straw that broke the camels' back to me was the successful attacks on my mental state and character that was alleged to be preventing me from being a good leader and competent pilot in the plane. I remember CDR F [redacted] saying to me at my second human factors board, in which he was the senior member trying to do everything to prevent me from discussing the safety information at the board, that it was essentially my fault that I found myself in this situation and essentially that I'd have been more believable if I hadn't given them so much to question me about my behavior. This was of course tough to hear because it suggested that I was failing at my pursuit of good and, shucks, I could've been successful if only I had handled things differently. I told the IG investigator during my interview that we all accept that at some point in the military we might be asked to have to be the fall guy or to jump on the grenade for something and sacrifice ourselves for the mission or perhaps the greater good but then I said that the situation turned a corner where it became clear I needed to think about protecting myself, the attacks against me were from within not coming from outside the wire. We get insider threat training all the time but were they all and the institutions behind them insider threats against me or did I represent the insider threat? That made the situation all the more surprising and confusing to me because we weren't dealing with classified information or a classified situation, just information about what was going on which people didn't want to get out to save face and protect their own butt. This happens all the time in the military, keep your mouth shut, group protectionism, but we were hurting ourselves here and protecting something, which seemed to me, that went against good order and discipline, departing from approved official standards and policy, and which was borderline criminal even before the attacks against me started. I was no longer acting to prevent bad things from happening, the grenade instead was coming after me and with a vengeance. So again, at this crossroads you can turn and run, which many people do and have, or you can continue fighting, or you can accept what they're saying and doing to you. Again, I think what motivated me to continue fighting was two things. The first was that the good intention behind all of this from the very beginning when I reported to the squadron and safety officer was to do the right thing, also for whatever the outcome of my efforts lead to something positive and make changes for the better through awareness and understanding based on truth, fact and reporting.

So is it understandable the way people in the squadron behaved and reacted to what I was reporting and the criminal decisions being made, yes. Did many of them behave wrongly and unjustly with their own interests in mind, yes. Are their actions, behaviors, and decisions forgivable, no. Am I trying to hold them and greater government offices accountable, yes. Was I successful at doing so, no. Is it important to understand why I wasn't successful, yes.

As it pertains to the story here, I could understand peoples' feelings towards coming forward and speaking out against certain behaviors, situations, and actions taken on behalf of the group that had become ingrained in the culture of things. At some point you feel like everything is O.K. and that you can keep on going, whatever is going on is working even though you know it's wrong or things are being done incorrectly. In this case it's not just an individual decision being placed upon you, it's a culture of attitudes that you're having to go against, for instance if there was another plebe also in my situation with the same sponsor so how would I have viewed the situation then or how would that dynamic have changed my decision. I don't think it would've changed my decision to not say anything but I do think if I did want to say something even though I knew things were wrong that it would've made it even harder to speak out. In these cases people's actions and decisions are understandable from that perspective but not forgivable. It's funny the justifications you make inside your head when perpetuating actions or situations that you know are bad. In the end however, this doesn't change the fact that the responsibility is there to speak out and if somebody is speaking out then the responsibility is there to support them and help them through it. For me at the squadron, the opposite was taken, I was cast aside like a dirty sock and made to feel as though I was crazy and acting crazy because I refused to perpetuate this bullshit situation of pussy leadership and a status quo of dysfunction in so many ways. It should've been enough for me to speak out on my own and people get behind me. In these situations it shouldn't be a popularity contest where I need to build a coalition in order to be heard about wrongful actions and behaviors. In situations like this for safety and reprisal the single voice should be enough. The way it's written, the policy and the law seem to have the correct intent to ensure this happens to where a single voice can rise to the top and be heard but regretfully the people and leadership in place to support it and the politics didn't support the corrective actions from being taken. ██████████████████████████████ ████████████████████████ My fellow officers and leadership, many of them should not have been allowed to continue in positions of leadership and many of them should've have been prosecuted. Simple questions to them, "Were you ordered from somebody higher in the chain to take those actions against me or did you make those decisions on your own?" "What were the interactions, conversations, communications/guidance between you and the chain of command about me and what I was reporting and what took place throughout spring, summer and fall before the complaint was issued and then after near the time I left the squadron?" "Did the IG ever interview you and what did you say?"

Complaint

What I didn't appreciate at the time about the complaint was that the government will follow human nature in most respects, follow the path of least resistance and if there's a way or loophole to follow to avoid having to do work then that's the path it will take. I naively thought that if I organized my materials like ***Mr. 5**** and **Special Agent 6*** at NCIS had suggested then the case would speak for itself because all the material is what I'd essentially gathered over the past year as the evidence, my circumstances in which I'd spoken out in a protected manner was pretty obvious and documented, and the acts against me as a result were so sloppily flagrant I don't know what else I could've presented to them to say "here's a serious problem, look at it." I was also naïve because I thought the IG and NCIS would be independent and do the right thing and look at the case before them objectively and if in doubt let the investigation run its course, grant a time waiver if necessary. Well the IG and NCIS were not independent and the investigation was never allowed to run is course so all that was left was my word and story against theirs. I still don't fully understand the meaning but the IG and BCNR appear to use a legal standard referred to as "regularity" which appears to place the burden of everything on the complainant.

I did not intend for my complaint to make me a whistleblower. To me I'd already let the safety information out of the bag so to speak and spoken out pretty forcefully so I was merely reporting on how it related in totality to the UPA's that were being taken against me while at the same time exposing the full truth of the safety story up the chain. Remember that, to me, my

complaint and the safety information and the story it told were like yin and yang, inseparable. I

initiated the complaint as reprisal against me for the safety related information I'd been

gathering, investigating, and reporting on and reporting up for more than a year and that I found

myself being stifled and muffled over for trying to do so as the depth of the safety violations and

causes became more comprehensive in nature pointing more towards a leadership failure by the

front office and other officers. The first written correspondence from the IG explained that case

moving forward would fall under the whistleblower protection program.

I was adamant about exposing leadership involvement in failures not just because many

of them were sons-a-bitches but more so because it was the true nature of the story. I remember

the CO's endorsement of one of the MISHAPS describing the primary cause as being over-

zealous young enlisted maintainers just wanting to do a good job at any cost or something like

that. First of all I felt like that was bullshit trying to pin the blame on the junior enlisted. Later I

saw the CO fire the maintenance Masterchief or I should say reassign to the same department I

was reassigned in the Mine Countermeasures Department. This was bullshit too because

somehow the culture and health of the maintenance department was being pinned on his back

when in fact I truly believe and think I've shown evidence of that he was unfortunately just

carrying forward and perpetuating an atmosphere and in many cases specific direction that was

being handed to him. For instance, I want you to follow all the rules by the book and don't do

anything unsafe but I want you to give me four "up" aircraft for tomorrow's flight schedule,

wink wink. I was simply trying to show how the dots connected all the way to the top which

they did and this was the fact that was most causal to everything going on and precisely what needed to be exposed for anything to change. The problem was that there were many more

than just him who apparently had their hands on the rudder of this boat who I was indirectly

speaking out against and I was about to get keel hauled.

NCIS

    I don't remember the exact time I went to meet with Special Agent 6 at NCIS. I put it

somewhere between September and October. When I went back several years later to ask about

our meeting I was able to remember his name and he was able to remember me and our

discussion so I know I wasn't crazy. At the time it was very hard to take this first step and I

thought NCIS was the first place I should begin because I felt somehow protected, that I'm not

doing anything wrong by going to talk to these guys who are supposed to exist to uphold the law.

I thought I was trying to uphold the law in that respect so I thought telling them the story of what

was going on and asking questions about what I should do was O.K. My trust for anybody at

that point was pretty tattered and I was honestly probably a little paranoid. He agreed the

situation was not right at all and that if I wanted to pursue some kind of action then the IG

sounded like the best people to talk to, but based on what he heard there were no specific crimes

in his jurisdiction that were / had been committed. I felt better but not completely satisfied. It

felt good to finally talk to someone but still it wasn't someone who could do anything about the

situation to help me. I still found myself alone and truth be told I felt very alone. In these

circumstances I can't really convey just how alone you feel but you find yourself on an island of

information that you probably can't talk to about with your wife, your friends, especially your

co-workers. Even when I was forced to go talk to the counselors at Portsmouth Naval Hospital

sure I felt better that I had cleared my chest with the story and telling him everything but all he could do to validate my situation was to tell the CO that I was cleared for full duty. So you're on this island surrounded by many people perhaps that want to help and agree with your story and would like to do something but just can't. And then there's friends and family who can listen, or maybe not, but definitely in most cases simply can't understand and they really can't help improve your situation either, maybe just provide moral support. You're in this situation and you know what you have to do and I can honestly say that it's not an easy thing to do to move this sort of complaint, or report, or action forward and take on the establishment which has more than enough resources to squash your balls into oblivion and make you go away, figuratively speaking, by keeping your voice from being heard. What humbled me always about all this that I recognized early on was that if in my position as an O-4 as a department head particularly as Safety Officer and it was this difficult for me to fight for what was right in this situation and speak out only to get shut down then how could anyone expect a junior enlisted in a similar situation to speak out about anything? This simply confirms my belief and insistence through this whole process that culture and command atmosphere is indeed a human factors related safety issue that needs to be scrutinized accordingly.

Three years after I submitted the complaint the IG finally reported back to me that my complaint would not be investigated due to the timeliness of when I submitted it relative to the last valid UPA (couldn't be more than 60 days I think). Important nugget and key takeaway for anybody in a similar situation.

My last FITREP they determined didn't count as a UPA because BUPERS said there was nothing adverse about it and was materially correct based on their guidelines. I found out much

later through the BCNR process that when I pushed back at this process to look at the validity of
the report in consideration of the full lens and context of my complaint and what transpired they
simply refused to do so stating that they are not an investigative body unable to make any sort of
determination in that respect so essentially all they could scrutinize and compare the process
against were the guidelines put forth by BUPERS. What a rotten fucking egg and self-licking
ass hole. The FITREP was adversely written and BUPERS and the BCNR fucking know it
whether their guidelines support it or not; the board can read between the lines of the report but
your process doesn't allow you to, that's bullshit.

There was another UPA that I included in my complaint; one the IG didn't even consider
which would have fallen within the 60 days. That had to do with my end of the fiscal year flight
time waiver.

After the IG finally got back to me (I'll say it again because I think it's ridiculous) after 3
years, they told me essentially the outcome and the reason and if I wanted to have the case
reopened I'd need to present new evidence supporting the validity of my case. I went back and
had that conversation with Special Agent 6 and communicated briefly on email up until the point where I
connected Special Agent 6 to the IG and then I was never able to reach him on the phone or email again. I
think I did try and go back to see him in person but when I did, he no longer was in that office or
was deployed or something. I felt like a stalker trying to get ahold of an ex-girlfriend.

IG

What can I possibly say about the IG? You know, it's funny I thought of this the other day. In trying to understand and answer the question why seemingly good intelligent people still get caught up in large numbers supporting bad group think, making bad decisions, and doing bad things? What I realized is that in addition to my other hypotheses throughout my story I think a principle reason for this is because they find themselves wrestling with the better between two evils in their mind—go against what leadership is telling them to do and follow my lead or not go against what leadership is telling them to do and support the status quo and make me go away. It's very possible that leadership above the CO and even the Commodore directed their actions against me to shut me up and run me out. That theory becomes more interesting later now that I think of it. Whether making the decision themselves or supporting a bad decision passed down to them I still hold the CO and his cohorts accountable and they're still a bunch of assholes for it. If there was specific direction from higher to take actions against me then I'd love to know about it. I wonder if this has anything to do why the case was never investigated? I'm pretty confident some of my fellow department heads felt like they had to choose between supporting me and my perspective vs the perspective of other department heads who they felt more loyalty towards for better or worse—stand by who's a better friend or more valuable to you not for what is right.

So for the IG, after consulting with NCIS on what I should do I contacted the IG office from the website over at USFF. Apparently the IG I contacted was actually the SURFLANT IG because their office was inside the old SURFLANT building now SUBFOR. Of course a lot of what I'm saying is repetitive from my report but since they won't simply publish my report I'm having to repeat myself. I still felt very uncomfortable and that I didn't fully trust myself nor the office I was consulting about my situation. Where I felt very safe about consulting with NCIS I didn't really have a warm and fuzzy about the IG because I didn't really understand what I was getting into and what the cost could be to me personally and professionally even though I believed I was doing the right thing by speaking out and pushing this situation up to the next level since I had reached a point with nowhere else to go. I essentially felt as though my chain-of-command had not only failed me but were so corrupt, dysfunctional, and misguided that only an independent outside organization could help objectively investigate, communicate the story and situation, and direct how to right the ship. I was wrong. From my perspective they were in on it from the very beginning. Maybe not all Navy IG or DOD IG but at least those members closest to the situation at AIRLANT and USFF. It's customary that entities be allowed to investigate themselves from within and accordingly it's unlikely that the chain-of-command is not going to agree with the recommendations and findings. I was disappointed though that even after the preliminary inquiry was released that the higher offices continued to insist that the process followed was correct, consistent, and didn't require further review. I'll never know really how far up the malfeasance of the case and the neglect of the "good process and intent" would go. I think in good government fashion at the time the higher up offices either just thought it would go away on its own like most of the cases do, and/or they just assumed that the work performed at the lower levels were just, verified, and in good order. So I don't think the higher offices set out to pursue negligence, although I don't know how you can reach a proper verdict on a case without doing a proper investigation. I think their negligence came after the fact when I started pushing back and of course now they needed to make a choice—look into the problem further or take the easy way out and perpetuate the poor choice of pushing me off at all cost. I remember talking with one of the representatives at the IG handling my case on the phone and her saying that she didn't think this sounded right and that she thought it would get looked into. This was a similar tune the IG rep from USFF told me over the course of the previous three years in which I was led to believe that due to the nature and evidence in the case that it would be recommended for full investigation. Later on, when I consulted the Congressional office the lady working for Steve Daines even told me that she thought that based on what I'd submitted that something didn't seem right here and that it needed to be looked into (not to get too far ahead but that didn't do anything neither). I thought since the process was taking three years that the full investigation was already taking place and the results I would be receiving had to do with a review and results of the full investigation of the case. I was wrong. I was finding that I continued to be wrong at many points along the way. Maybe I'm wrong for writing this? I look forward to the day that one of these assholes says, "You know what Zach, you were actually right, and we were fucked up." That ain't going to happen. We fight for what we believe in and if it's right and just, then keep fighting because the people and organizations against you are never going to admit fault or change because it's not within their political will nor interest to do so. When you make the choice to be an outsider of wrong-doing, stand-the-fuck-by, cause you ain't getting back in. So at this point I thought I had the support of some people still in the squadron, I thought NCIS had endorsed my effort, I thought the IG was taking care of business and doing the right thing in my defense and to correct the safety wrongs, and I felt good that even if the case and results didn't find me vindicated then at least I felt like it followed its due course and I could accept the results. Well the case was never investigated so I had to continue fighting for some kind of closure to the situation and correctness to the wrongs not just I felt against me but towards truly exposing the true nature and reality on the ground of what had been going on and what had been leading to the MISHAPS and negative culture within the squadron, later to be exposed across the community. That made everything even more surprising because after I left the squadron, many independent reports concluded similar if not exactly the same findings across the community and program enterprise not just within our squadron. Not to mention the reporting later from Wes's story. It was as if the leadership didn't want anybody exposing that they as an enterprise may have known just how fucked up they were ahead of time and therefore were unaware to do anything about it. And that there was nobody in the system speaking out. Well I was speaking out, I did speak out, bad things started to happen, they started taking things out on me for it for continuing to speak out, bad things continued to happen, they refused to acknowledge connection with me and any of the dots, they refused to accept any culpability, and the IG of all people who by design should be able to intervene chose to do absolutely nothing. So fuck you guys!

I sort of digressed. When I showed up for my initial meeting with the IG I was still reluctant about what I was doing, if I was going about things the right way, was I doing something wrong by taking this step (knowing in the back of my head that there would be a point where once I opened the can of worms there would be no going back for me, I would be in it till the end without really knowing what was going to happen). There was also just the doubt in oneself associated with knowing that you're choosing to go against the "man" and the organization. In the military you're brainwashed early on to always support the chain-of-command and protect the commanding officer. There was a strange feeling of doing something unnatural and that I was really going to have to commit to this, go out on my own, and that the gravity of it was not going to be easy. Was I doing the right thing and were my reasons for doing so legit and not just because like they claim that I was a disgruntled employee or because I simply had personality differences with a bunch of those sons-a-bitches. Basically I really had to overcome the doubt in whether they were actually right about me which was a really shitty position to be in on top of the position I was in. Whatever they might do to fuck with you and try and shut you up it can be pretty damn effective and for myself who I considered to be fairly strong willed and stubborn I can only imagine the personal inertia and reluctance the average person might feel to come forward let alone fight and fight and fight to report and expose something. Even now writing all this thinking about it is not easy and they succeeded in making me question myself, making my family and friends question me, making my professional life question me. The one belief though that was and has been solid throughout though is that I know it was and continues to be the right thing to do and that my intentions remain the same and true.

I encourage you to question me as well so I can share this truth with you, or just take my word

for it here through my report.

So did I submit my complaint at that first meeting with the IG? Hell no, I did not. My

instinct about the situation and the people I met with was that something wasn't right or that I

just wasn't ready to move forward, they jumped into wanting me to commit to signing a bunch of

stuff and I balked. I felt kind of like I was the one being questioned and about to be investigated.

I left with being directed over to the AIRLANT IG ▮▮▮▮▮▮▮ since I was reporting a
Mr. 5

squadron matter.

I called up ▮▮▮ and scheduled a meeting. I believe that the first phone call I made came
Mr. 5

from my office because I couldn't find it in the phone record for my cell phone for that

timeframe. This became an issue later when they wanted me to verify that I had submitted my
Mr. 5

complaint earlier. Regardless, I went in and met with ▮▮▮ and told him everything and that I

anticipated based on what was going on that the actions towards me would be extended into

affecting my FITREP. Now, clearly it did negatively and adversely impact my FITREP even

though I've had BUPERS twice or more tell me otherwise that it simply didn't meet thresholds

for "adverse." It was just a little too convenient however that I was supposed to receive my

FITREP on Oct 31 but I didn't receive mine until about 30 days later. ▮▮▮ advised me to go
Mr. 5

ahead and wait until I received my FITREP to submit my complaint so I didn't submit until early

December. I'm curious what the communication back to my CO from AIRLANT was about the

complaint they were about to receive and whether there was any guidance provided about my

Mr. 5

case that I had previously revealed to ████. Well we'll never know because they wouldn't

answer my questions about it and the IG refused to look into it once I called their bullshit.

Fuuuuck you!

Transition

Mr. 5

After submitting my report to ████ detailing my complaint and the situation and history

of what had been going on, I heard nothing until January. I waited through my remaining time at

the squadron in awkward malaise with CO and other department heads not really being able to

reveal openly what I had done. They all just pretty much left me alone it seemed but I'm pretty

confident most people knew that I'd dropped a formal complaint. Normally a department head

leaving the squadron is pretty smooth and traditionally the front office will have communicated

or at least gone to bat for you with Placement and the detailer to give you the best orders

possible. Well I wasn't hearing shit and I had been negotiating some crazy scheme to go to the

Indian War College. Now just as I was about to commit to the orders somebody gave me some

good gouge that made me hold off a little but around that same time I got called into the CO's

office. This was probably February I think because it was after I'd been interviewed by the IG in

January. The CO told me that I'd been asked to take a job over at USFF and that he highly

recommended that I take it. Well thank you CO for that incredible detailing advice. I didn't

have much to say in response, I wasn't provided much detail just that it was some kind of special

project. I said yes.

Period 6 May2013-May2016

USFF

My orders had me detailed to leave the squadron that spring and check into USFF before heading to the new operational planner's course in the fall. The new training program fell somewhere between the master's level training and the elementary level training currently being taught. Graduates from this course were supposed to I guess serve as the continuity workhorses across the staffs that could translate and get done the important work between the detailed planning of the masters and the snapshot understanding of the grade-schoolers. We were to fill an important gap within the Fleet to provide a broad knowledge base for the planning process and how to get things done the right way within the larger joint and maritime planning process. I'd been previously indoctrinated into the military planning world from the assignment I had in Germany for eight months where I learned how to be a missile defense planner within the larger joint planning process across EUCOM.

I started out on the watchfloor to get qualified before heading to the training. When I got back I was assigned to one of the back offices to go to work. We started an exercise almost immediately after checking into my new planning job so I spent a week finishing my paperwork and then went onto the night rotation for the exercise.

Admiral name

The most interesting thing I can recall about my interactions with ADM ********* (*callsign*) was something he said during my first IPR (Intermediate Planning/Progress Review). He called us into his office and he quickly went around the room for introductions saying "I know you," "I know you." When he got to me I introduced myself and that I flew 53's and just checked onboard from HM-14, and he said that "oh yes" he remembered me. When he shook my hand and greeted me he said very solemnly that he was sorry and that's not the way things are supposed to happen at the squadron or something to that effect. He didn't directly address me or the situation concerning the complaint but for me reading between the lines that's what I thought he meant by the statement and apology, and still to this day that's the only bit of recognition and apology from the chain-of-command about what transpired and the report I submitted that I ever heard. I didn't mince words in response. I simply said "yes Sir" and we proceeded with the meeting.

I gotta rewind a little. While I was in the planners course **Admiral name** came to visit the class since we were the first "Beta" version of the course as it was being rolled out so to some extent everybody attending was somehow handpicked for it. For me I don't know whether it had to do with my unique planning background or if it had anything to do with the IG complaint. When **Admiral name** spoke to us we went around the room and had the chance to introduce ourselves, say what command we were going to, and ask a question. For me I told him that I was coming to work for him as his new planner (since I was the only one assigned to USFF) and I asked him if he could tell me what project I'd be working on when I checked in. I think I caught him off guard with the question a little but he told me that he thought I'd be engaged somehow with the work we were doing with climate change.

I was on the night watch after beginning my new planning job back at USFF. An exercise was underway, I'd only been there about two weeks. I was not a climate change planner but instead was assigned as the DSCA lead. It's not important you know what that is, just that I was a planner working in the plans shop. I was about a week into the exercise when I showed up for work that afternoon to start my shift as an OPT lead. I started getting these messages that everybody had been looking for me, "where have you been" people kept asking. I finally saw

somebody who told me that they'd been looking for me all day because the COM was looking

for me and that they needed me to start this new job right away. I finished my shift that night,

leaving a little earlier I was told I needed to report to the N8/9 in the morning to start my new

job.

I was apparently by name request by COM as the new planning lead to develop the EMW

Campaign Plan. One major problem starting out is that nobody could tell me what EMW was

and what the campaign plan was meant to do. Be that as it may I was presented a great

opportunity and honestly I was too busy at that point to really care or think about anything else.

The position started out in the N8/9 which if you don't know what that is then don't worry about

it, not important but I went from a world of likeminded planners working together and wanting

to get stuff done to the opposite extreme of bureaucratic processes and staffs not wanting to work

together and slow rolling any possible opportunity to do good work for the greater good of the

service if it at all threatened a particular rice bowl of money. So that critique is done. EMW

lead planner and planning team lead was actually a great job, opened lots of different

connections and challenged me in new and interesting ways that I appreciate now. The work

though was definitely not as fun or exciting as flying. I made some good friends from the N8/9

and I felt like generally they were all good people trying to do good things. The work brought a

different type of stress that I seemed to be pretty well at handling because nothing we did on the

staffs was going to kill you but I felt good about the fact that by doing a good job you would help

divert war or prevent war #1, preserve life if war is necessary #2, and if an adversary must be

defeated by brute forced capitulation then it would be done swiftly and decisively #3. I wouldn't say this ethos matched everybody else's that I worked with but at least that's what kept me going. Today my hope is simply that I'm able to apply my strengths, skill, and intellect towards something other than the teaching and practice of disciplined warfare as I'm tired of trying to change and influence a system of people and processes insistent upon undisciplined warfare. Succeed and overcome the enemy at any cost doesn't mean doing so by ignoring doing the right thing, neglecting to properly understand who the enemy is in the first place, not willing to say openly in a position of leadership and responsibility that the emperor wears no clothes, pinning your organizations mistakes and failures on the backs of those who work for you especially the most junior, and refusing to recognize that the enemy might be yourself. That's enough pontificating.

AIRLANT

Admiral name decided relatively quickly that the effort and leadership behind it needed to reside elsewhere so he tapped**Other Admiral** to carry the water. The effort went from a one star up to a two star with me as its principle. There were several staffs in between with many O6's who were eager to get a piece of this pie, some more than others. For me it meant undesired notoriety and attention. This was problematic for me in many ways but primarily because I didn't work for any of them and they didn't work for me but I was somehow supposed to streamline some kind of unity of effort around developing this supposed campaign plan. My chain of command was not clear but if I had to guess at that point I'd say that I reported to the N8/9 and his deputy and then directly to COM. At AIRLANT this didn't change except that now I was reporting to **Other Admiral** directly and then to COM. It was also problematic because I'd been put in charge of a job that many of these other individuals and staffs should have all been doing in the first place, and they didn't want me involved, so I had to also encourage and foster their involvement and willingness to take it over eventually. For the most part I got along with everybody but there were a small number I butted heads with. So I spent about a month sitting in my cubicle running things out of the N8/9 and then abruptly was reassigned and sent over to AIRLANT to take up shop and continue running with this football. AIRLANT seemed definitely more my people and I enjoyed the working environment much more for some reason, I felt a little more protected by those above me. I kept on churning, got some messages pushed out and kept trying to do what I thought **Admiral name** wanted through his and the CNO's vision. In this position I felt very much like a target from many different angles but I recognized that it was very unusual to find yourself in a position such as this as an O4 with as much leadership opportunity and responsibility and influence over the major decisions and mechanisms that make the Navy go. Not to mention, and that many people warned me about, once people discover a particular initiative is important to the boss then that immediately translates itself to money being spent and everybody wants to get their piece of it so in some cases everybody now wants to be your friend and sell their great idea under this new umbrella regardless of its usefulness. Generally everybody was very excited about lending a helping hand and enthusiastic about what needed to get done until you start handing out work to do and assignments and looking for answers to tough questions then everybody disappears. Part of this was simply that people were afraid to sign their bosses up for a work assignment that may not be within the appropriate lane nor the ability to accomplish. Either way this work was challenging but many things, not all, got accomplished. I stuck with it as best I could but I felt many of the other staffs simply were not taking things in the direction the COM nor the CNO wanted. **Other Admiral** was preparing to present the campaign plan to COM and the CNO and I was very dissatisfied with the progress and the shape others were trying to make of it. My job title was not so clearly defined but one of them was clearly executive assistant to the admiral so in this executive assistant role to **Other Admiral**, he called me in for a one on one discussion about the product prior to the brief and asked me what I thought because I seemed frustrated or dissatisfied with it. I simply told him that I thought it was a mistake to try and sell this product to COM and the CNO as the campaign plan or going in that direction, that it wasn't what they wanted nor envisioned, and at best the brief should simply be an update to the progress. The reason this was important is because there had been a timeline given to the effort and the campaign plan was supposed to be completed. **Other Admiral** agreed and changed the brief to reflect that it was just an update and they would need to further discuss where to take things from there. I enjoyed working for and with **Other Admiral**, *COS* and the rest of the staff.

NWDC

I was at AIRLANT for about 6 months before the next change. COM decided NWDC would now be the one to carry the water and move the effort forward as the campaign plan began transitioning into an implementation phase. I'd pretty much had enough of wrestling some of the people and forces involved in the process. I found in some ways I think many people felt like my position and influence was more of an impediment for the effort moving it forward. I'd become more of a quality control fixture for the admiral as an executive assistant or personal advisor than I was a planner. When I checked in with Sterno upon arriving over at NWDC to my new cubicle he called me in for a one on one and basically asked me what I thought and how things were going. I told him that progress was being made slowly and that there were many people and staffs within the process that would just like to see it go away or who are just taking every opportunity to slow roll everything from moving forward. He surprised me with his next question by asking me who exactly was slow rolling the progress. I actually withdrew a little at his question which seemed to turn him off a little, as if now I could find myself protecting bad actors, but I said that I couldn't say that it fell on a specific individual or set so I simply described some of the interactions between the staffs and what their interests seemed to be. This answer did not seem to completely satisfy him but I'm not sure exactly what he thought I would or could actually reveal, as if I could analytically explain why and by who the campaign plan was taking a back seat or failing. I may have just read too much in it. Either way, after that it seemed that Stearney was intent on taking things from there and I was happy to see him do it but to do that meant that I would begin taking a backseat myself. As I was still technically in the chain of command to **Admiral name** I continue to inject myself when and where I felt it was necessary, getting yelled at for it at times, but for me and my role I was intent on seeing through my original purpose I thought which was to help ensure and see through the COM's and CNO's vision for EMW and the campaign plan. Many at that point were satisfied to see the effort die on the vine so to speak but I continued to highlight the key points of the effort that still had not been completed per the original intent of messages released by COM. Most of these had to do with assessment and I'll just leave it at that. I spent the next several months in a tiny room with several other people developing something very few believed in. I was happy to see it become many years later the assessment strategy for the CNO's Fleet Design.

Congressional Inquiry 1

By this time in the back of my mind I was always wondering what was to come of the complaint I filed and what if any tie to it did my current job and situation have to it? Three years had almost passed since the original submission. My quasi EMW lead planner billet had been officially given a position, title and billet number at NWDC but I would no longer be filling it.

They handpicked somebody new to come in and fill it. I was satisfied with what I had

contributed and accomplished at times it seemed doing the work of an Admiral, Captain, and

Commander all at once with little to no authority to do either. I'd developed strong relationships

with all the staffs I worked with and for the most part I think I'd earned respect from a lot of

people but at the end of the day when it was all done I was still an O4 with no real job or title no

longer with a by name request from COM to protect me. Despite my best efforts with solid

FITREPS from several admirals along the way I'd still failed to promote. My best chance came

while under **Other Admiral** but still my situation leaving the squadron could not be

overturned. I had originally asked ADM **Admiral name** to sign my FITREP since I was his

by name request and technically worked for him at USFF but I was shot down. I also asked if

Admrial name would provide me with a letter but a captain in his office told me that he

wouldn't allow him to entertain my request because then he'd have to do it for everybody

regardless of the circumstances. I don't think ADM **Admiral name** actually ever received

my request about the FITREP or the letter. Apparently there were a lot of others higher rank

than me who were also interested in a bump from ADM **Admiral name** so I was just

another name in the back of a long line. Why had I been afforded this incredible opportunity?

In some ways I felt like yes it was a great leadership opportunity but in other ways it seemed

that I was being put in an impossible position to fail, be closely monitored, be scrutinized, and

then if the results of the investigation were in my favor then they could sing my praises and call

it a success and if not then it would be the perfect opportunity to continue discarding me since

I'd spent the last three years in a billet that didn't exist doing work that largely didn't exist to

anybody or that nobody really recognized. USFF could also make the argument that I had been

afforded the most career enhancing opportunity to

succeed and promote and if I didn't then it was on me and not them as a counter to my reprisal

case. I tried not to waste too much time thinking about all of it but I can't deny it crossed my

mind. This was all simply conjecture and nobody was ever going to tell me one way or another.

It could make you paranoid if you dwelled on those thoughts long enough. Something else I felt

like was that while I appreciated the opportunity in some instances, I felt I was actually the one

under investigation through all of this and constantly under the microscope. Now, I didn't mind

working my butt off, contentious staffs working late, technical staff work and constant analysis

that would make you want to gouge your eyeballs out sitting inside cubicles all day with no

windows. I did get the feeling though that I was still having to prove myself and justify what I

had done. They were somehow making me prove my worth by putting me in this goat rope of a

position. Whether my CO was at fault or somebody above him told him to take those actions

against me to shut me up, he was still the one responsible for carrying out the actions. I was

hopeful and confident that the complaint was being investigated and I like to believe that if

investigated I would have accepted the results regardless of whether they were satisfying and in

my favor. The fact of the matter was at the end of my EMW days was that nothing was going to

correct the damage of my paperwork leaving the squadron. I was now simply a somebody with

bad paper, unusual paper, but still bad paper who had dropped a complaint and was sour about

the outcome. As I went through those three years following my department head tour I

discovered the real concern was not about promotion nor complaint, it was actually whether I'd

be allowed to retire. At one point I remember questioning whether I'd be granted continuation

to even make it to retirement which unfortunately directly impacted my GI Bill transfer of

benefits to my kids by being denied. After being passed over for O5 a second time the process

required my record to be reviewed for continuation since I had not made it to 18 years yet.

Obviously I did get continued and I did retire but for a short time there existed the possibility

that I was going to be forced out of the Navy in 6 months and with the results of the complaint looming I had little confidence that anything at that point was guaranteed. While I was working

hard at my job I was also very frustrated that I was dealing with those realities and the realities

and conditions for being passed over for promotion. This was all even before I'd received the

results from the IG. On top of everything else at that time I applied to transfer my GI Bill

benefit to my kids following all instructions given to me but, due to an administrative error

processing my request because continuation didn't allow a page 13 to be filed, it was denied.

What I'd come to find out later was that, while I was struggling and working my butt off

at my job hoping that the IG was doing good work looking into the infractions carried out by my

CO and company, nothing had actually been done to that effect. These guys were getting a pass

while I was rubbing elbows with the admirals having to justify my existence to them under

impossible circumstances. Now I don't want to sound bitter and unappreciative of these and

other opportunities, but let's be real. What I was finding in the squadron was becoming true

even now. No matter what I did performance wise there was no way I would recover and remain

competitive in the process. The CO was determined to taint my record and that's what CDR A

and CDR D did. Now they'll argue that it was within their right to do so within the established

rules and guidelines for commanding officers. Of course, like I've said in my report several

times, this is true but it cannot be as an extension of a punishment for speaking out about wrong

doing and especially not due to an aggressive record of speaking out for safety related issues. It

was as if I had made all this up, I'd put it all there in the report, did the IG not read it? What was

even more frustrating was that the official record of my FITREPs was only one small part of the

punishment to my professionalism and my career. As if the FITREP was the only litmus

representing the standard or threshold that needed to be crossed in order to establish wrongdoing

against me by those individuals as a UPA.

Up to that point I had been assigned to USFF the entire time filling a billet in the operations department as a Battle Watch Captain. I had been reassigned three times internally from the N32, to the N8/9, to AIRLANT, and lastly to NWDC. Even more strange was that suddenly they cut me new orders within my current set of orders to have me officially gained by NWDC and to fill one of their billets in OPS. I spent about a year in that job. Talking before about being under immense scrutiny during my time at USFF in that unique position. Not just due to the clearance level requirements but I felt like I was constantly being set up for something. While jokingly, they had me in unusual capacities that would make security managers cringe. At one point I had permanent access badges to three different commands floating about freely between meetings, running meetings, etc. It would have been extremely easy to take advantage of the situation because there was no one person over me that really knew where I was supposed to be and when. It would have been very easy to get in trouble or misstep in a hundred different ways whether through security violations or otherwise trying to wrangle all the moving parts and discussions. I thought I did pretty well given the circumstances. I took it as a sign of great confidence and trust in me but couldn't rule out totally being set-up also. It's always possible too that they set me up intentionally expecting me to fail or misstep along the way and I actually ended up being successful so they didn't know what to do with me, "shit this guy just won't go away." So I slide into my new cubicle position at NWDC and have a new set of bosses who still really don't know what to do with me. I helped and seemed to do some odd jobs here and there supporting different efforts but basically my greatest contribution it felt like was on the Gatorball field. I enjoyed the people there and we had some good times and I like to believe we did some good work. Stearney continued doing his thing carrying the water for EMW as I watched the struggle continue from the sidelines. I still take a little pleasure knowing I had to pass the full effort of EMW lead over to Stearney as a two star. This may be a little of an exaggeration but that's how it felt to me.

Stearney turned over to *callsign* **Another Admiral** just before I checked-out. I'd put EMW behind me but always wondered what would come of it and whether I had helped even a little advance the COM's and CNO's vision for it. It was during my remaining time at NWDC when I received the results from the IG concerning my case. What I submitted had morphed into many different names in my mind. Initially it was a safety report, then it became a complaint, then it became a reprisal complaint, then it became a whistleblower complaint, then it became an IG investigation, then it became simply my "case." Later it became a congressional inquiry twice then it became a BCNR case twice then it became just me talking to myself here. Each step of the way I built on it with new information but from the beginning my case was always based on the same set of initial information from the safety reports. After fighting unsuccessfully with the IG about the results I had received the two options presented were to file a BCNR request to officially change my record and/or submit my case for congressional inquiry. So I did both since nothing I was going to say or do was going to change the IG's mind. So now I was taking the fight to a new level. I wasn't just saying that the squadron leadership was screwed up, I was suggesting that Navy and DoD IG were screwed up and complicit. I think the process is designed to wrestle you into submission by waiting you out. Pessimistically I was not confident any of it would amount to anything. The first BCNR request seemed a bit fanciful but I figured if I'm going to do this I'm going to ask for everything and if it sticks then I would want the response to me to be big.

There was no way anybody now was going to side with Me following the decision by the Navy

IG and endorsed / approved by DoD IG.

I just kept submitting the whole report with every submission so I was hopeful that

somebody along the way would actually read it and take action on it. With each new request I

tried to tell the story over and over again hoping something might stick but it wasn't enough, just

the usual "yeah that really sucks man, sorry but not my problem, guidelines weren't necessarily

violated, nobody did anything illegal, not worth the time to look into further." Each time I would

have to wait 9 months to a year for a response. I left NWDC in October 2016 not knowing what

was going to happen.

Period 7 May2016-Oct2017

Bahrain

I was excited to leave NWDC, not because of the people but because of the job. I'd been

there way to long and no matter where I moved I couldn't escape the reality of the crazy situation

I was in without any real insight as to why—only my own thoughts and wasted postulations. Not

to mention you reach a point at any job in the Navy where you know it's just time to move on,

you've overstayed your welcome. I tried to leave HM-14 early when I was there and it was clear

I was just treading water. I think around the time after they officially took me off the DET OIC

rotation, not really sure though. I'd found a great job at the Australian War College in Canberra

and I think I would have had to leave like three months early. Nope, wouldn't support me going.

Were you keeping me around to be your scapegoat? If my job was so critical and you liked what

I was doing so much why not replace me with one of your golden boys. I thought I'd give him an out and let me go away gracefully. Who knows, I probably would've. Was it all part of his plan? Was he intentionally keeping me there to do this job because he knew nobody would do such a good job as me and that I was the only one that was going to get to the bottom of things and reveal the true picture of what was going on? Well so where did I go wrong and why did you take those very overt actions against me clearly designed to intimidate and shut me up? I just don't know either.

I was pretty shook up before getting to Bahrain. About two weeks before catching my rotator I was half asleep on the couch with my wife watching TV and suddenly a strange feeling came over me and my heart started racing uncontrollably. I thought I was having a heart attack but the ER determined it was a panic attack. Either way it sucked and introduced me real quick to the realities of stress and living with some degree of anxiety disorder. I'd never experienced anything like it. I never had any problems compartmentalizing stress or just accepting things as they came. I'd never reacted to anything stress related physically in that manner. It was very uncomfortable and mixed with depression is very scary because you know you don't feel good and you know something is wrong but you don't know what it is nor how to fix it. You're just stuck struggling inside yourself. I started talking to the counselor before I left for Bahrain and followed up my appointments with the counselor in Bahrain. I was able to manage and work through it with help from the counselor and leaning on my friends from work but it definitely opened my eyes to a new reality I was going to have to learn to live with for the rest of my life. I don't know what caused it or what would trigger it. I did some self-study and realized, at least for me and my situation, non-hypoglycemic low blood sugar mixed with diet and lack of exercise seemed to have a lot to do with it. The symptoms would seem to come and go, when it hit me the worst the condition seemed almost debilitating. An attack would hit me at the strangest times, usually not anywhere near the crazy stress of work most of the time just walking around and during down time sitting in my flat. Almost always when I didn't have anything else to distract me and I'd have time to dwell on the reality of being away from home and not having access to my family. Depression definitely became mixed into the equation which I think led to the debilitating episodes where I'd find myself just walking around the base on a weekend buying groceries and it seemed the walls would start to just close in around me and I'd become very scared and alone feeling like I was going to die for no reason just by standing there. It would make you freeze and seem like it was difficult to move. I'd work through the episode by identifying it as such and doing my self-talk and breathing to just continue. I'd sit down or sometimes force myself to keep walking with an objective in mind to simply make it back to my room and try and focus. I talked to the counselor several times about the episodes and how I was feeling. Obviously the question of whether you had thoughts of killing yourself was asked. I had to consider the question because I wanted to make sure that if I needed more help then I could take the appropriate actions to deal with it, but I determined that and I was confident that how I was feeling did not include desires of killing myself but I could definitely relate to the physical pain some people describe when they get very depressed to the point where for no reason the pain inside physically hurts and you almost feel desperate to just want to make it go away. So in that sense I could relate to a very small scale the gravity of what could lead to suicide if not properly identified early and dealt with properly. I told work what was going on, not in stark detail, but about the appointments to talk to somebody and I was having to work through some things. Work was no problem, I had a good relationship with the boss and most of my cubicle buddies, and my contribution was solid and respected, I was still able to perform and actually wound up excelling in most respects at work with the exception of dealing with one personality conflict with another one of the planners. All in all work seemed not the issue though and while work was definitely a contributing factor since the nature of the work was very stressful and the reason for being in Bahrain in the first place I realized deep down the symptoms were related to dealing with issues at home and the separation. I hadn't been deployed for a very long time before that, pretty much since 2003 and that was only for 5 months. This was for a year and I was having to basically get back up to speed with it real quick, basically strengthening my composure along the way. In the end my time in Bahrain was great, very challenging, I learned a lot professionally and personally, made some great friends, unfortunately did more drinking than I should, and learned some things about how the world works that opened my eyes in good ways and bad. I should also give a shout out to my friends from Montana Em, Lori and Claudia and their dog Libby who has since passed. I always tease Em that his dog likes me more than him. But when I needed them they were there for me and it was great having the opportunity to visit them on occasion while I was over there and shed some of the turmoil I was feeling, so thank you.

██████████████████████████████ We struggled through it and will be fine

but it comes at a cost for the individuals and your relationships with them. Luckily our friends,

neighbors, and family provided her with a similar outlet as did Lori and Emerson for me.

In any case, the symptoms were the worst during periods of downtime where I didn't

have the stress of work or something else distracting me. I also found if I skipped breakfast and

had gone without eating a meal for long periods I would start to feel anxious and potential onset

of an attack. And when I started running and exercising again it seemed to make the physical

symptoms lessen or just made me physically more able to absorb the stress related illness.

As far as what I did at work, we did what you do as a military planner—we planned on

how to kill other military forces in the quickest most effective way possible and meet our

national objectives in the process. While things didn't work out for me as a department head,

I've turned out to be a damn good operational planner. I just wish that my skill was more

focused on figuring out ways how not to kill people but that is the reality for the military, this is

what we do.

BCNR 1

About halfway through Bahrain I received word about the Congressional Inquiry and the

BCNR I'd submitted. Basically the Congressional Inquiry did nothing but to ensure the BCNR

request would be accepted and a board would review my case. The BCNR results did nothing

but to tell me that the board of three members reviewed my case and determined the FITREP in

question was good without any fallacy associated with it and that the requested change to the record was denied. What was unique about this BCNR was that the request was actually submitted by Senator Steve Daines' office so I can only assume that the entire case and all the enclosures were included. Based on the BCNR's response I surmised that the board didn't actually review the case and all the information in its entirety whether they actually received it or not. I believed they issued a "verdict" based solely on review of the FITREP in question and the determination by the DoD IG regarding my case. The FITREP would not seem unusual without putting it in the context of the case in its entirety during the marking period in question. The case in its entirety would likely not be reviewed to understand the full context if you only stopped once you saw the determination made by the DoD IG that the case was not valid due to the reporting delay and therefore not investigated. I had a hunch a minimum level of effort had been applied by the board to review my full case and therefore I called their bullshit.

Congressional Inquiry 2

This time I submitted the Congressional Inquiry with the BCNR request as an enclosure and sent the request also directly to the BCNR for review so there could be no question regarding the information I wanted reviewed and the associated nature and context of my request. I continued to present and argue my case the best I could clearly laying out all the relevant facts, circumstances, and timelines. I tried in several different ways to present something that seemed very crystal clear to me but for some reason nobody on the receiving end would take time to review, understand, and take appropriate action to investigate and resolve.

BCNR2

I received the response back from Senator Daines' office that there was no further action that could be taken as a result of my inquiry other than to await the results of the BCNR. I then, just this past August 2019, received the final results of the BCNR. They made it clear, in the letter at least, that the board members reviewed the case information in its entirety and regretfully still determined there was nothing materially wrong with the previous FITREPs per their guidelines. They also said basically that while the additional information I provided was important it was not applicable to making their determination as they are not an investigative body and they are not allowed to make any determination based on such information. They also denied my request for a special selection board since no change to the record was necessary.

Period 8 Oct2017-31Jan2020

FACSFAC

My organization here in the manuscript experienced a little bit of time warp since I'd been at FACSFAC a while and had not received the results of the second BCNR yet so I need to rewind a little. After I submitted my last Congressional Inquiry and BCNR I pretty much new that was my last hurrah trying to properly utilize the existing process to support my case and finally investigate my complaint. I knew that for the BCNR to rule in my favor they'd essentially be accepting fault for the Navy that not only had a mistake been made, a correction necessary, and subsequent special selection board which might likely promote me, but the mistakes had been made based on a complaint they must find valid and therefore go against and reverse the determination and mistakes made by the DoD and Navy IG's not to mention fault placed on my CO and the behaviors in the squadron. For the Congressional Inquiry to get more involved there needed to be more of a political will in the fight which my case simply didn't have to garner more support. I wasn't making them more money, influence, or more votes I suppose. I was in a situation where the government could have its cake and eat it too at all levels because I'd handed them the information they needed to internally manipulate changes to the program without repercussion or accountability while keeping me silent since technically all this information is controlled by a non-disclosure agreement the IG had me sign at my first interview. Oops. I guess they'll have to come after me now. I'll thank the President for providing the necessary precedence here to speak so crassly and openly in supposed violation of established policy about an illegal NDA and the information it was supposed to protect and the people and players involved at the core of this story.

I left Bahrain in October 2017 and checked into my twilight tour at FACSFAC VACAPES. The job was great, the people were incredible, and I couldn't be happier how my retirement came to a close.

Waiting

In the back of my mind, like so many times previously, I always wondered about the possibility of what would or might happen with my complaint and the results of the BCNR.

Retirement

I was happy about retirement. I felt good about the ceremony and I felt satisfied about what I'd accomplished over the course of my career. I still felt like I had a lot to offer but I was one step closer hopefully to fishing full time with my kids and maybe grandkids out on the lake with worms and catfish charlie. People always told me beforehand that I would reach a point in my career when you just know you're ready to retire. I reached that point out in Bahrain while walking into work one morning. A strange sense of calm came over me and I knew I was ready and wanted to do something else. A satisfied feeling came over me that I could really contribute no more to the Navy and I could move on. The feeling I felt as a Midshipman that kept me going and prevented me from leaving all this time until I knew I was ready had finally hit me and I knew it. Amidst all the uncertainty about what was going on I felt certain about being ready to retire.

I cried like a baby up on the stage and some people were disappointed because they wanted to hear more of my speech. This manuscript is why you couldn't hear more of it until now. We would've been there awhile plus not the right venue. My guest speaker captured the moment extremely well and even touched on a little of this struggle as "speaking truth to the man," thanks for that.

Results

So now what? I've got the results. I'm at the end of my rope. What the hell am I supposed to do, walk away? What more can I say about it here? Well, I uh, well…didn't do anything, right away. So much time had gone passed but to me I could still recount much of what happened and my feelings towards it with great clarity. Of course I was upset, but not surprised for the many reasons already mentioned. Of course in the absence of a true investigation of the truth this manuscript is my last attempt to make sure the information gets out there for public consumption and awareness about what happened and what I experienced. It may be a little raw and not the best written but that's part of the story since I didn't set out to be a novelist, or whistleblower, or to come into odds with my CO and have to fight him and the rest of the establishment over something which to me is blatantly obvious as not good leadership, wrong, unjust, and criminal in the big picture. At a minimum I'd fire every one of those motherfuckers from the squadron all the way to the top but I'll have to settle for this reprimand. What about wholeness for the whistleblower? Getting these words out there is the best I will get to repair the damages left behind. As part of the deal I will continue to receive unwanted and undeserved scrutiny and attention for something I did not perpetrate nor ask for. I will continue to be the bad guy and that is simply the life story of a whistleblower that you will need to accept once you stick your neck out there. They will certainly not let this go and I guess I won't neither. They will continue to fight it and say they were justified in their actions and decisions and that I should just learn to be satisfied and to stop being so disgruntled and bitter. A simple sorry and thank you would suffice for me. To be truly honest, maybe a little money and a promotion would have been nicer.

Contracting

It became clear after about three months that I needed to start working again. Contracting in this area is a logical choice for somebody in my position plus I needed a job quickly. Didn't take long and essentially I was back doing the exact same thing I was used to doing before but just as a contractor. Thoughts of the investigation still loomed in the background but the ball was in my court. I took my time and tried to gain some perspective.

Copyright office

Even before I received the final letter about the BCNR results, I rather quickly started organizing my complaint and materials after the retirement ceremony and started trying to put the story into some kind of organized narrative. I printed a copy to see what it would look like. I sent a copy to the copyright office. Their response was a little surprising but the work could not be copyrighted because they considered it a compilation of working papers or something like that so it would not qualify as a manuscript or original work. The copyright office simply declined it in a letter.

FOIA

This took a little longer, but I wanted to see if what the last BCNR said was true. I wanted to see if they'd actually received the full report and if all the material was actually included in the case and reviewed. I expected to see a full FOIA copy of my complaint as it was submitted. I have no way to verify that the board actually reviewed and took the case information into account when making their decisions. It appears at least that most of the case material was included in the review package as I had submitted it. There does appear to be some additional information included as correspondence between reviewers about the case but still not substantive regarding details about how the reviewers felt about the case and the contents and merits. I think their summary letter pretty much described how they felt about it which is that they are not an investigative body so nothing in the additional case information was really relevant even though in my view the context of the complaint is everything. The reviewers had it in their power to do more and they chose not to. Everybody along the way including the congressional offices had it in their power to do more and they chose not to.

Book

I eventually realized that if I wanted to publish anything then I'd need to start writing it down. I started working but many problems still haunted me on the horizon. How do I publish without getting sued? Do I try and make money through the book? What do I do with the profits? Do I self-publish or try and go through a company? I dug a little and thought if USNI was willing to publish it then that would be a logical choice since to me this was a Navy related matter that the Navy needed to come to terms with and begin setting the example and lead the change necessary to fix peoples' attitudes towards the subject. What subject? Well I suppose if I had to summarize the theme beyond my report and this short synopsis then I guess I'd choose being able to recognize doing the right thing and being courageous enough to do it and support it over personal self-interest, loyalties, biases, and group think. I remember a friend of mine after the fact, a fellow department head at the time, who told me later that I probably deserved being promoted more so than he and that he remembered them asking him about the situation, knowing full well most of the details since we had many discussions about them, and he basically said that well Zach just seems to be having a tough time with things but "this person" didn't really know what it was all about or something to that extent basically taking a pass. Well for this individual and others who openly passed up their opportunity to speak out even when asked about it all I can think about is when GOT character Cersei Lannister does her walk of shame. Don't worry about it, that's O.K. dude, thanks I got this. Although reprimanding him here, I didn't reprimand him then because while not O.K. I could understand, simply not forgive. His greater loyalty was to his other friends I guess who were also department heads. To back me he'd have to essentially be calling them liars and backstabbers. My message to everybody is that someday you will have to choose which backstabber is doing the right thing and which one you will have to choose to get behind. As one of the JO's told me who worked in the safety office before I arrived, "I did my part." I had asked whether anybody prior had been working to update the safety program instruction. This person had made the updates, gave it to the department head and never followed up when it didn't go anywhere. Do the right thing next time and do more.

Closing

I want people who read this to understand my story and how it's impacted me and my family. I want people to learn from it. I want leaders to read it and think twice about how and why they're making certain decisions about how to respond to certain people about how they're acting and why and what steps to take, and to not simply use the analysis here in this manuscript to more adeptly circumvent future instances in a more closeted and criminal manner to more effectively put a muzzle on it. I want this story to build awareness and generate useful discussion about the issues being raised here. I want it to help the study of leadership among future officers and government leaders. I want this story to create a perspective and backdrop for understanding the errors in community and program culture and atmosphere that could have been corrected by leadership and standers-by early on if they'd only listened, and how these corrections might possibly have broken up the Swiss cheese from forming just enough to have prevented the unnecessary deaths of our friends and loved ones. We can't bring people back but we all have an opportunity to make a difference and I hope this makes even a small difference. I also want to convey a sense of damage that we all have experienced at one time or another that leaves a permanent mark on us somehow mentally and perhaps physically in some cases. We all have "stuff" we're dealing with, currently or in our past, and I don't want to minimize other people's stuff nor make it out that in some way my stuff is somehow more important that I've chosen to speak about it in this manner. Many of us have been damaged in our own unique way under differing circumstances. After 20 years in the Navy dealing with this and other issues I can convey a sense of damage that I've left behind through writing this to a certain extent but much of it remains. Maybe it manifests as anxiety or maybe it's a twitch or a stutter some discomfort that escapes explanation but you know it's there. Despite the damage, the accusations, the paranoia, the damning, the praise, the death, the victory and the fallout, underneath it all is only one truth: I had to do what I did and there was only one way to go about doing it; I had to go all the way with it no matter what that meant to me personally or professionally. I did the right thing and I was punished by my chain of command and others for doing it, and was wrongfully and unjustly attacked in a manner that was professionally harming, malicious, systematic, coordinated, intentional, and shameless—in a manner that is criminal by all definitions of statute and elements of the law. If for no other reason these individuals who kept their mouths shut or perpetrated these offenses did so in violation of good order and discipline, following orders that were unlawful, and giving orders that were unlawful. These crimes were further perpetuated by higher offices through complicit coordination or negligence of the offices they were there to represent. These crimes and the fallout that resulted in death and destruction along the way are attributable to all of the failed leadership involved therein. You know who you are and you must now own the damage of that forever.

     To hell with and fuck the naysayers—"Well he deserved it, he's a piece of crap, he doesn't know what he's talking about, he should've and should now just keep his mouth shut, we had it all under control and he was the one that went off the reservation by openly going against the CO by being outspoken and insubordinate, everything he says just proves that we were right and justified in our response in how we handled him and the situation regarding the community's safety apparatus, leadership, and operational culture."

I truly still think that these individuals still believe that early on when I was just getting started they figured well let's give him a chance, if nothing else he'll just bury his own grave and if he is right then it makes us look good that we supported him. I think they thought that they could just keep me and the developing situation in a box. I think the CO figured as time went on and it was clear after the MISHAPS that the situation was not going to be contained that he could suddenly turn around and say that look at all these things we were doing to prevent this situation from occurring and here are the reasons why and what we're doing to fix it. I think what my analysis clearly conveys and what this shouting continues to be about is the cover up of the true reality of the situation and the causes behind what was going on to create the hostile atmosphere, maintenance malpractice, acts of reprisal, and simply the human factors that led to the MISHAPS in the first place which I believe includes the factors that led to the other MISHAPS across the community at the time and extends to Wes' as well. All these issues and factors were not isolated in a vacuum and unrelated, they were all an extension of the same bad practices, culture, and leadership failures, period. That's what should've been in the reports from the beginning stemming back to my initial reporting and that's what should be in every report now as fact plain and simple so I hope you take the time to read everything and see if you agree with me. As far as why I took the next step to defy my CO so aggressively in seemingly clear insubordination and contempt, well because he wasn't doing the right thing (in many respects as a shitty Skipper) by specifically not conveying to leadership the true nature of what was going on, and had been. Well shoot what did I expect that he would tell on himself—yes I did and when he didn't and I called his bullshit he came after me with clear intent and action to put me down and take every administrative action he had at his disposal against me to the max extent possible within the supposed guidelines. Many believe it's within every Skipper or commanding officer's right to suck or make those decisions that make it a shitty place to work and to serve while under the guise of accomplishing the mission but I don't believe this is true if the decisions or complicitness in the lack thereof come at the illegal expense and safety of his or her people. You know if you want to fuck me administratively and sink my career opportunities for promotion then do it for the myriad of other things going on by others in the squadron at the time like the OIC sleeping with a junior enlisted, chain of command sleeping together out on DET, simply doing a shitty job as a pilot department head and officer, but you'd better have clear grounds for your actions and decisions. I don't believe clear and justifiable grounds for the actions that were taken against me include my aggressively speaking out about and pushing to expose this information. I'd love for them to show me how it does and if not, if the actions were perpetrated on other qualified grounds, then I'd love for them to show me what those were. The explanation presented to me at the time during the human factors boards and the formal counseling was complete bullshit and all these fake and orchestrated hearings refused to acknowledge my case, and the whole process since then perpetuated this refusal to acknowledge my case and justify the actions and characterizations taken against me in my FITREP and other documents. You can believe what you will but I will not allow these conditions to continue to be levied upon me and my character without making my case. I fought back and was defeated in that respect, but here's my story about it to tell my side and expose what I believe is the truth about what happened and what I was fighting for and what he and the rest of the chain of command didn't want exposed about how fucked up they were and most likely continue to be, refused to own up to it as leaders, and pinned it on the backs of junior and senior enlisted, and told me to fuck off for it. Well I'm finally getting to say Fuck You to them and make my case in the process.

The only true measure that will substantiate my case and subsequent story will be those involved and witnesses coming forward and speaking out too. What would you do in this situation and how would you handle it?

Books 1 & 2 are free to the public to read at
www.goodleaderslost.com

<u>The following pages are provided</u>

2020
31Jan2020 Manuscript proposal   p. 107
Apr2020 FOIA POC correspondence   p. 108-111
Feb2020 USNI correspondence p. 112-113

2019
9Sep2019 final BCNR response Ltr p. 114
27Jul2018 BUPERS response to BCNR p. 117-122
Aug2018 and Sep2019 BCNR POC correspondence
1Oct2019 initial copyright office response p. 123

Misc
23Jun2016 Tester response Ltr p. 125
7Jul2016 privacy release for Tester p. 126
17Jun2016 privacy release Daines p. 127

Publishing Proposal for Manuscript

January 31, 2020 at 3:05 PM

Clarence Zachary Graves

Virginia Beach, VA 23455

Word count: roughly 20,000
Page count: roughly 50 pages (manuscript), reference documentation includes roughly an additional 150 pages

Leaders Lost is a fresh and sobering first-hand non-fiction account of one man's challenges when faced with reprisal being forced upon him by his aviation squadron CO and further exacerbated by a negligent Navy, government IG, congressional office, and several other Shipmates who stood by while it happened. The scene of the story takes place over the course of about eight years and documents his journey through the trials and tribulations of backstabbing, bureaucratic nonsense, and the twilight zone of reasonably good people insisting upon knowing what the right thing is to do and then doing the exact opposite. Leaders Lost represents a play on words where the Leaders that became Lost for political reasons and not having a spine directly contributed to the decisions and conditions set into motion which led to some incredible Leaders actually being Lost in unnecessary and preventable aircraft MISHAPS. His vitriol towards detrimental status quo and those that support it refreshes the instincts to once again question authority especially when it's tough. At its heart however the story shows the importance of believing in yourself, not giving up, and trusting in those that help and support you to get you through the hard times.

Clarence Zachary Graves retired on 1 June 2019 after serving 20 years on active duty in the United States Navy. He still works for the government as an analyst, planner, and executive team builder.

FOIA No: 2020005072
30 Mar 20

MR CLARENCE Z GRAVES

██████████████████

VIRGINIA BEACH VA 23455

Dear Mr. Graves:

This is in reference to your request, pursuant to the Freedom of Information Act (FOIA), 5 U.S.C. 552, and Privacy Act, 5 U.S.C. 552a, tracking number DON-NAVY-2020-005072, for "BCNR case files for Clarence Zachary Graves BCNR Docket numbers 4304-18 and 8863-16 and IG case numbers 201602083 and 201300109 to include BCNR board member names and how they voted.

In this regard, a copy of your BCNR file has been uploaded to DoD SAFE at: https://safe.apps.mil . I have emailed the access information, including the password, to your ██████████████████ account. Pursuant to exemption 5 U.S.C. § 552 (b)(6), names and other personally identifiable information have been redacted where indicated.

You also requested the names and votes of the Board members. For docket number NR20180004304, Ms. *.████████ Ms. *.██████████████ and Mr. *.████████ were members of the Board who unanimously denied your case. For docket number NR20160008863, Mr. *. ██████████████&, Mr. *.████████ and Ms. *.██████████████ were members of the Board who unanimously denied your case.

Please note that this Board does not produce or maintain the IG records as described in your request. There is no central Freedom of Information Act (FOIA) processing point for records for the Department of Defense (DoD). FOIA processing is decentralized and delegated to those officials of the military departments and various DoD Components who generate and or maintain the records being sought or reviewed. In consideration of this fact, we advise that you submit a FOIA request to the IG office in procession of the records you seek.

You may appeal this response to the Department of the Navy, Office of the Judge Advocate General. Please be advised, however, that your appeal may only concern whether our office has provided you an adequate response to your Privacy Act request (i.e. a challenge to the adequacy of the search) the Office of the Judge Advocate General has no authority itself to reconsider or overturn the BCNR's decision denying your petition. An appeal under the Privacy Act may be made in writing and sent to:

Office of the Judge Advocate General
General Litigation Division (Code 14)
1322 Patterson Avenue, SE, STE 3000
Washington Navy Yard, DC 20374

Any appeal must be postmarked within 90 calendar days from the date of this letter and include a statement explaining why the appeal should be granted, a copy of this letter, and a copy of the original request. Both the appeal letter and the envelope should bear the notation, "Freedom of Information Act Appeal." Failure to include this information could result in the Department's rejection of your appeal.

If further inquiry is required regarding this matter, please contact me at ██████████████████@navy.mil. You may also contact the DON FOIA Public Liaison, at ███████████████@navy.mil, or (703) 697-████.

                    Sincerely,

                    ████████████████
                    Government Information
                    Specialist By direction

I'm trying to access the DoD Safe files but it's not letting me do so through my iPhone. Are there specific browser requirements? It's telling me that it requires a secure connection. Thanks.

R/ Zach

Sent from my iPhone

On Apr 2, 2020, at 4:30 PM, ██████████████ CIV USN BCNR WASHINGTON DC (USA) ██████████@navy.mil> wrote:

> Mr. Graves,
> The responsive records to your FOIA request have been sent to you via DoD SAFE. The information to retrieve your records is detailed below. Please let me know if you have any questions.
>
> URL:
> https://safe.apps.mil/pickup.php?claimID=96rYMWN6FdohoCuD&recipCode=N4hRn4
> Passphrase: Gr@v3s_5072
> Claim Passcode: 9a86Y4XeYEpYdfVV
>
> V/R
> Ms.████████████
> Government Information Specialist
> ⚓ Board for Correction of Naval Records
> o: (703) 604-████ e:████████████
>
> FOR OFFICIAL USE ONLY - PRIVACY SENSITIVE: ANY MISUSE OR UNAUTHORIZED DISCLOSURE MAY RESULT IN BOTH CIVIL AND CRIMINAL PENALTIES.
>
>
> <FOIA 2020005072_Graves, Clarence (BCNR records, names, votes)_response.pdf>

Sent from my iPhone

Begin forwarded message:

> **From:** Clarence Graves <████████@██████.com>
> **Date:** April 3, 2020 at 12:20:28 PM EDT
> **To:** ████████████ CIV USN BCNR WASHINGTON DC (USA)" ████████████@navy.mil>
> **Subject:** Re: [Non-DoD Source] Re: FOIA Response: DON-BCNR-2020-005072

Got it downloaded thanks.

R/ Zach

Sent from my iPhone

On Apr 3, 2020, at 10:19 AM, ████████████ CIV USN BCNR WASHINGTON DC (USA) ████████████@navy.mil> wrote:

Good morning Sir,
I have not tried accessing the site through an iPhone, but I suggest trying from a computer if possible.

DoD SAFE is a secure site, and has specific requirements to ensure safe transfer of your records.

V/R
Ms. ████████████
Government Information Specialist
⚓ Board for Correction of Naval Records
o: (703) 604-████ e. ████████████@navy.mil

FOR OFFICIAL USE ONLY - PRIVACY SENSITIVE: ANY MISUSE OR
UNAUTHORIZED DISCLOSURE MAY RESULT IN BOTH CIVIL AND
CRIMINAL PENALTIES.

From: Clarence Graves <████████@██████.com>
Sent: Friday, April 3, 2020 10:07 AM
To: ████████████ CIV USN BCNR WASHINGTON DC (USA)
<████████████@navy.mil>
Subject: [Non-DoD Source] Re: FOIA Response: DON-BCNR-2020-005072

Cc: Submissions, Press <PressSubmissions@usni.org>
Subject: Re: Your manuscript submission to the Naval Institute Press

Thank you ▮▮▮▮

The manuscript is only about half done with much more to be written, reaching the 100,000 word count should not be a problem. What is the next step here if you are interested? I think there will also be additional information provided in the length of the forward that I don't have yet. The story continues to evolve but my part is pretty much wrapped up and that is what I'm writing about. Thanks for the speedy response.

R/ Zach

Sent from my iPhone

On Feb 12, 2020, at 3:15 PM, ▮▮▮▮▮▮▮▮▮▮ ▮▮▮▮@usni.org> wrote:

> Hello Mr. Grave,
> Thank you for taking the time to contact the Naval Institute Press regarding your manuscript. As described, the manuscript would be far too short for us to consider at 20,000 words. The majority of our books are 100,000 words or a bit more.
> However, I want to wish you the best as you pursue other publication options.
> Thanks and kind regards,
>
> ▮▮▮▮▮▮
>
> ▮▮▮▮▮▮▮▮ | Acquisitions Editor, Naval Institute Press
> U.S. Naval Institute | ***************@usni.org
> (o) 410.295.▮▮▮▮
> www.usni.org
>
> <image001.png>

To: Clarence   **Cc:** Press

Hello again,
We would be happy to review the full manuscript when it's completed, as long as it's much closer to 90,000 or 100,000 words.
All the best,

************************ | Acquisitions Editor, Naval Institute Press
U.S. Naval Institute | *************@usni.org
(o) 410.295.1067
www.usni.org

U.S. NAVAL INSTITUTE

The Independent Forum of the Sea Services

See More from Clarence Graves

****

Docket No: 4304-18
Ref: Signature Date

LCDR CLARENCE A GRAVES USN
****

VIRGINIA BEACH VA ******

Dear Commander Graves:

This is in reference to your 8 May 2018 reconsideration request. You previously petitioned the Board for Correction of Naval Records (Board) and were advised in our letter dated 5 September 2017 that your application was disapproved. Your case was reconsidered in accordance with Board procedures that conform to *Lipsman v. Sec'y of the Army*, 335 F. Supp. 2d 48 (D.D.C. 2004). After careful and conscientious consideration of your new and material evidence or other matter not previously considered by the Board, the Board found the evidence was insufficient to establish the existence of probable material error or injustice. Consequently, your application has again been denied.

Regarding your request for a personal appearance, the Board determined that a personal appearance, with or without counsel, will not materially add to their understanding of the issues involved. Therefore, the Board determined that a personal appearance was not necessary and considered your case based on the evidence of record.

In your previous petition to the Board (Docket #8863-16), you requested "all adverse, derogatory and/or questionable misrepresentation/reflection of my performance associated with or as a result of the information presented in and/or investigation results from Inspector General (IG) cases 201602083 and 201300109" and "congressional inquiry response dated 12 July 2016 be modified in a way that properly reflects/represents my performance and/or simply removed and replaced by an official letter signed by POTUS explaining the reasons for the errors, purpose for the letter and how the errors are adequately corrected through the intent spelled out and explained in the letter." You contested the validity of your fitness reports (FITREPs) issued during the period from 1 November 2011 through 22 May 2013, and requested the convening of a special selection board (SSB).

Your application has been carefully examined by a three-member panel of the Board sitting in executive session on 16 July 2019. The names and votes of the members of the panel will be furnished upon request. (Instructions on requesting your BCNR case files are available at https://foiaonline.regulations.gov/.) Documentary material considered by the Board consisted of your application and any material submitted in support of your application. The Board also considered the enclosed 27 July 2018 advisory opinion (AO) furnished by the Navy Personnel

Command (PERS-32) and your rebuttal of 31 August 2018. Although the Board determined that you did not submit any new matters with your application, it considered your case on the merits because it previously did not render a decision regarding your request for an SSB, and because you contend that FITREPs not previously considered are also in error and unjust.

Your current petition requests that the FITREPs issued at HM-14 be removed, replaced, or fixed to accurately reflect your performance at the squadron—specifically, to include your high water competitive FITREP to reflect verbiage showing the strongest recommendation for promotion to commander and aviation operational command. The Board noted that this request includes two additional FITREPs, issued during the period from 18 March 2011 to 31 October 2011, that were not previously considered by the Board.

The Board, however, substantially concurred with the AO that nothing in your petition substantiates your claim that your Reporting Seniors (RSs) acted for illegal or improper purposes or that your FITREPs lacked rational support. Forced distribution limits the number of "Early Promote" and "Must Promote" recommendations in a summary group. You were ranked in competitive peer groups ranging from six to seven members, and it was within your RSs' authority to rank each member based on their observation and determination, and within the guidelines of the EVALMAN. You were under the observation of different RSs, and your ranking for each FITREP was consistent. Your promotion recommendation on the first three FITREPs was Promotable, and you improved to Must Promote on the next report. Your final FITREP was a "detachment of individual" report in which you received an Early Promote recommendation. Additionally, the trait grades, comments, and promotion recommendation assigned on each report are not adverse, and you were graded at or above standards.

You also request the Board include verbiage in your record showing and describing the errors and injustices that the Board's corrections overturn and why, and include as part of the record an understanding of who the primary offenders were, their names, what role they played in the offenses, and any outcomes in their dispositions from any proceedings, and for the Board to solicit a more thorough explanation about why the Navy IG did not fully investigate your case, and why the Navy IG or Department of Defense IG did not waive the time requirement.

The Board, however, did not find any probable material error or injustice. Moreover, the Board is not an investigative body. The function of the BCNR is to consider applications properly before it for the purpose of determining the existence of error or injustice in the naval records of current and former members of the Navy and Marine Corps, and to make recommendations to the Secretary or to take corrective action on the Secretary's behalf when authorized.

With regard to your request that an SSB be convened, the Board determined that, because your record was not in error or unjust, an SSB is not warranted.

It is regretted that the circumstances of your case are such that favorable action cannot be taken at this time. You are entitled to have the Board reconsider its decision upon the submission of new and material evidence, which will require you to complete and submit a new DD Form 149. New evidence is evidence not previously considered by the Board. In this regard, it is important to keep in mind that a presumption of regularity attaches to all official records. Consequently, when applying for a correction of an official naval record, the burden is on the applicant to demonstrate the existence of probable material error or injustice.

Sincerely,

9/9/2019

X *********

****
Executive Director
Signed by: **************

Enclosure: NPC memo 1610 PERS-32 of 27 Jul18

1610
PERS-32
27 July 2018

MEMORANDUM FOR THE EXECUTIVE DIRECTOR, BOARD FOR CORRECTION OF
NAVAL RECORDS

Via: PERS/BCNR Coordinator (PERS-3C)

Subj: LCDR CLARENCE Z. GRAVES, USN, XXX-XX-

Ref: (a) BUPERSINST 1610.10C (EVALMAN)

Encl: (1) BCNR File NR 4304-18 wo/Service record

1. Enclosure (1) is returned. The member requests all fitness reports while assigned to HM-14 be either corrected, removed, or replaced.

2. Based on our review of the material provided, we find the following:

   a. A review of the member's headquarters record revealed the fitness reports ending 19 May 2011, 31 October 2011, 10 May 2012, 31 October 2012, and 22 May 2013 to be on file. Each fitness report was signed by the member acknowledging the contents of the fitness report and his right to submit a statement. The member indicated on each fitness report except the report ending 31 October 2012 that he did not intend to submit a statement. For this report, the member's statement and the reporting senior's endorsement are not present in the file.

   b. The fitness reports in question are all reports issued to the member while assigned to HM-14. The reports were submitted for various occasions from different reporting seniors. The member alleges that the fitness reports do not accurately reflect his performance and requests they either be corrected, removed, or replaced.

   c. The fitness reports are valid reports.

   d. Fitness reports are unique to the period evaluated. Per reference (a), chapter 2, page 2-1, paragraph 2-3, a CO may submit properly authorized FITREPs, CHIEFEVALs, and EVALs on any individual, regardless of rank, who has reported to that CO for permanent, temporary, or ADDU under competent written orders. Each fitness report was accurately prepared and submitted by the reporting senior in accordance with reference (a) for the occasions indicated.

   e. Reference (a), chapter 1, forced distribution, limits the number of Early and Must Promote rankings in a summary group. The member was ranked in competitive peer groups ranging from six to seven members and it is within the reporting senior's authority to rank each member based

AUG 1 6 2018

on his observation, determination and within the guidelines of reference (a). In this case, the member was under the observation of different reporting seniors and the member's ranking for each fitness report was consistent. The promotion recommendation on the first three fitness reports were Promotable and the member improved to Must Promote on the next report. The member's final fitness report was a detachment of individual report in which he received Early Promote as the only member in the group.

f. Reference (a), page 9, paragraph 15, requires the member to sign all of their Regular reports, unless impossible to do so, and shall sign other reports where possible. The member shall receive a copy of every report from the reporting senior at the time it is signed. The member has the right to submit a statement to the record concerning their report, either at the time of the report or within 2 years thereafter. In this case, the member had the right to contest each fitness report at the time of issuance by submitting a statement or using other avenues to resolve alleged inaccuracies or discrepancies on the reports. The member only indicated on one report the intent to submit a statement, which is not on file. Each fitness report in question greatly exceeds the 2-year period from the ending date of the report.

g. The evaluation of a member's performance, the member's standing within a summary group and corresponding promotion recommendation are all responsibilities of the reporting senior. It is not uncommon for members to disagree with their reporting senior's appraisal. In this case, the fitness reports are administratively and procedurally correct based on the requirements of reference (a). The trait grades, comments and promotion recommendation assigned on each report are not adverse and the member was graded at or above standards.

h. In reviewing petitions that question the exercise of the reporting senior's evaluation responsibilities, we must determine if the reporting senior abused his/her discretionary authority. PERS 32 cannot comment on the reporting senior's intent for the fitness reports in question or what input they received just the foundational elements of the fitness report as it applies to the instruction. For us to recommend relief, the petitioner has to show that either there is no rational support for the reporting senior's action or that the reporting senior acted for an illegal or improper purpose. Nothing in the member's petition indicated the reporting senior acted for illegal or improper purposes or that the fitness reports lacked rational support.

i. PERS 32 found the evidence insufficient to establish the existence of probable injustice concerning the alleged fitness reports.

3. We recommend the member's record remain unchanged.

By Direction

from my iPhone

n forwarded message:

From: Clarence Graves <_______@___.com>
Date: September 11, 2019 at 4:04:34 PM EDT
To: "___________CIV USN BCNR WASHINGTON DC (USA)" <_______@navy.mil>
Subject: Re: [Non-DoD Source] BCNR CASE #4304-18

Thank you.

Sent from my iPhone

> On Sep 11, 2019, at 3:51 PM, ___________ CIV USN BCNR WASHINGTON DC (USA) <_______@navy.mil> wrote:
>
> Good afternoon,
>
> Your case is in process, and you should receive your decision letter within a few weeks.
>
> v/r,
>
> _________
>
> Senior Examiner, Performance Section
>
> ⚓ Board for Correction of Naval Records
>
> o: (703)-_______ | e: _______@navy.mil
>
>
> FOR OFFICIAL USE ONLY - PRIVACY SENSITIVE: ANY MISUSE OR UNAUTHORIZED DISCLOSURE MAY RESULT IN BOTH CIVIL AND CRIMINAL PENALTIES

1

-----Original Message-----

From: Clarence Graves <________@____.com>

Sent: Wednesday, September 11, 2019 3:34 PM

To: ********* CIV USN BCNR WASHINGTON DC (USA) <********* @navy.mil>

Subject: [Non-DoD Source] BCNR CASE #4304-18

Hi *********

Can I please get an update on the status of the subject BCNR case #? Thank you.

R/ Zach Graves

Sent from my iPhone

from my iPhone

forwarded message:

From: Clarence Graves <__________@_______.com>
Date: September 10, 2019 at 11:45:49 PM EDT
To: _________@_____.com
Subject: Fwd: BCNR CASE #4304-18 ADVISORY OPINION

Sent from my iPhone

Begin forwarded message:

> **From:** "___________ CIV DONAA, BCNR" <___________@navy.mil>
> **Date:** August 29, 2018 at 1:34:58 PM EDT
> **To:** "________@_______.COM" <________@______COM>
> **Subject:** BCNR CASE #4304-18 ADVISORY OPINION
>
> LCDR Graves,
>
> This is in reference to your application for correction of your naval record.
>
> The records in your case were referred to the appropriate offices for an advisory opinion. This opinion has been received and is enclosed for your information. This opinion is advisory only and not binding upon the Board or the Secretary of the Navy.
>
> If you wish to submit any further statements or additional documentary material in support of this application, you should do so within 30 days from the date of this letter. Communication via e-mail, directly to my e-mail address (___________@navy.mil) is preferable. Unless you request a written extension of time within the 30 day period, this case will be decided on the evidence of record as soon as a crowded docket will permit.
>
> Please don't hesitate to contact me if you have any questions.
>
> V/R,
> Ms. ____________
> Board for Correction of Naval Records
> Naval Support Facility

1

701 S. Courthouse Road, Suite 1001
Arlington, VA 22204-2490
☎ 703.

United States Copyright Office

Library of Congress · 101 Independence Avenue SE · Washington DC 20559-6000 · www.copyright.gov

October 01, 2019

Clarence Graves

Virginia Beach, VA
United States

Correspondence ID: 1-3QANGU4

RE: Leaders Lost and 1 Other Unpublished Works

Dear Clarence Graves:

We are writing to refuse registration because these works are not eligible for the Group Registration of Unpublished Works application.

A group of works may be registered using the Group Registration of Unpublished Works application if all of the following eligibility criteria are met:

(A) Each work in the group is unpublished;

(B) The group contains no more than ten works;

(C) No compilations, collective works, databases, or websites are included in the group;

(D) A separate title is provided for each work in the group;

(E) Each work in the group is uploaded in a separate electronic file;

(F) All the works in the group were created by the same author or the same joint authors, and the author and claimant information for each work is the same;

(G) Each work in the group is registered in the same administrative class;

(H) The group is assembled in an orderly form and the works are submitted in an acceptable file format.

The works submitted are ineligible for registration using the Group Registration of Unpublished Works application because the work titled "Leaders Lost" is a compilation of emails, letters, memoranda, reports, and other documents in violation of requirement (C).

You may reapply for registration at any time by submitting the appropriate application, fee, and deposit. In all cases, the required filing fee and appropriate deposit copy of the work must accompany a new application. If you reapply, please disregard the attached reply sheet.

Or, in the alternative, you have the right to appeal our refusal to register your claim as submitted. To do so, you must submit a request for reconsideration along with the $250.00 filing fee. If you request reconsideration please follow the instructions on the attached reply sheet.

Please note that the filing fee for this application is non-refundable.

This letter is for your information only; no response is necessary.

Sincerely,

Literary Division
Office of Registration Policy & Practice
United States Copyright Office

Enclosures:
  Reply Sheet

JON TESTER
MONTANA

COMMITTEES:
APPROPRIATIONS
BANKING
INDIAN AFFAIRS
VETERANS' AFFAIRS
HOMELAND SECURITY AND
GOVERNMENTAL AFFAIRS

SENATE HART BUILDING
SUITE 311
WASHINGTON, DC 20510
202-224-2644
INTERNET:
http://tester.senate.gov/contact

United States Senate

June 23, 2016

Clarence Graves

Virginia Beach, VA

Dear Clarence,

Thank you for contacting me about your issue with the Navy. The Privacy Act of 1974 requires me to secure your written consent prior to any advocacy on your behalf.

Please fill out and sign the enclosed form, which will enable me to conduct an inquiry on your behalf and return the form to:

> Office of Senator Jon Tester
> 130 W. Front St.
> Missoula, MT 59802

Be sure to include any additional information that would help me assist you. Because I cannot guarantee the return of any original documents, you should send copies. If you have any questions, please don't hesitate to call my office.

I am honored to be able to assist you.

Sincerely,

Jon Tester
United States Senator

Jon Tester United States Senator for Montana

Case Information and Privacy Act Release Form

The Privacy Act of 1974 is a federal law designed to protect you from any unauthorized use and exchange of personal information by federal agencies. Any information that a federal agency has on file regarding your dealings with the United States government may not, with a few exceptions, be given to another agency or Member of Congress without your written permission. Family members, friends, or other interested parties generally may not authorize on your behalf the release of information covered by the Privacy Act.

Full Name: Clarence Zachary Graves

Date of Birth: [redacted] E-Mail Address: [redacted]@[redacted].com

Address: [redacted]

City: Virginia Beach State: VA Zip Code: [redacted]

Day Phone: 757 [redacted] Eve Phone: [redacted]

Social Security Number: [redacted]

File or Case Number: IG Case # 50.41/201300109

Federal Agency involved in your case: DOD - USN

I hereby request assistance of the Office of Senator Jon Tester to resolve the matter described on this form. I authorize Senator Jon Tester and his staff to receive any information they might need to provide this assistance.

The information I have provided to Senator Jon Tester is true and accurate to the best of my knowledge and belief. The assistance I have requested from Senator Tester's office is in no way an attempt to evade or violate any federal, state, or local law.

Signed: [signature] Date: 7 JUL 2016

Please state your request and a brief explanation below. Attach **copies** of any documentation which may help resolve your case. Please do not attach original documents, as we cannot guarantee their return. Feel free to use the back of the form if you need additional space. Please print or type.

See attached letter dated 26 May 2016. Please also confer w/ Senator Daines' office who has also responded to my request. Ms. [redacted] military representative from his office has been in contact w/ me. 406-493-[redacted] [redacted]@daines.senate.gov Thank You ~/Zach

United States Senate

Due to the provisions of the Privacy Act of 1974, (Title 5, Section 552A of the U.S. Code), permission in writing is required before making an inquiry on your behalf. Completing and signing this form authorizes U.S. Senator Steve Daines and those acting on his behalf to make inquiries to the appropriate federal agency on your behalf. Your signature also gives U.S. Senator Steve Daines and those acting on his behalf permission to send a copy of this form and any attached letters or supporting documentation to the appropriate federal agency. Then return this form to:

U.S. Senator Steve Daines
Attn: Constituent Services
104 4th Street North, Suite 302
Great Falls, MT 59401

PH: (406) 453-0148
FAX: (406) 453-5379

Clarence Zachery Graves
Your Name – Please Print

Date of Birth

U.S.
Country of Birth

Street Address or Post Office Box

Apt/Suite Number

Virginia Beach
City

County

VA
State

23455
Zip Code

757
Home Phone

757 341 4086
Work Phone

757
Cell Phone

Social Security Number

IG Case #5041/201300109
File/Case Number (if applicable)

17 JUN 2016
Date

@   .com
Email

Signature* (Required)

Please list, if any, family members with whom my office may discuss your case?

Wife: Graves

Please list the *Federal Agency* involved: DOD – USN

Explain your situation with the above Federal Agency. Use the back side if necessary:

See attached letter dated 26 May 2016.

Leaders Lost Series Book 2

Appendix B

Government record of reviewed files

Redacted Name List and Meaning in no particular order:

Mr. 1

Mr. 2

Mr. 3

Ms. 4

Mr. 5

Special Agent 6

Mr. 7

Ms. 8

CDR A

CDR B

LT C

Ms. 9

Mr. 10

CDR D

CDR E

CDR F

Books 1 & 2 are free to the public to read at
www.goodleaderslost.com

Public service cannot be selfless and self-serving if it seeks to promote yourself or build yourself up by tearing others down in the name of protecting the organization or just following rules or orders; that is not sacrifice, that is shitty, and selfish, and should be prosecuted. For something greater than ourselves, the Constitution or the greater good, you must find the light that it represents and pursue it while being able to discern the difference between the shadowy temptation vs the storm clouds over the path less taken. Either way there is always something to learn but you have to want to understand and find the greater good, not just follow blindly. Think hard, Act better. The shadowy path towards temptation is an illusion that will lead you astray, but you can always recognize it and follow the storm clouds towards redemption anytime; no matter what, the path will not be easy nor should it. This is life.

www.ingramcontent.com/pod-product-compliance
Lightning Source LLC
Chambersburg PA
CBHW081356150726
48196CB00005BA/520